158.128 Cortland, Sherri, 1957-
COR Spiritual Toolbox
12/13 FRA

# S L
# TOOLBOX

Are you ready to put on your BIG Lightworker pants?

Sherri Cortland, ND

ST. MARY PARISH LIBRARY
FRANKLIN, LOUISIANA

© 2013 by Sherri Cortland
All rights reserved. No part of this book, in part or in whole, may be reproduced, transmitted or utilized in any form or by any means, electronic, photographic or mechanical, including photocopying, recording, or by any information storage and retrieval system without permission in writing from Ozark Mountain Publishing, Inc. except for brief quotations embodied in literary articles and reviews.

For permission, serialization, condensation, adaptions, or for our catalog of other publications, write to Ozark Mountain Publishing, Inc., P.O. box 754, Huntsville, AR 72740, ATTN: Permissions Department.

**Library of Congress Cataloging-in-Publication Data**
Cortland, Sherri, 1957-
*Spiritual Toolbox*, by Sherri Cortland
Compilation of tools available and necessary for the lightworkers during the ascension.

1. Ascension 2. Lightworkers 3. Spiritual 4. Metaphysics
I. Cortland, Sherri, 1957- II. Spiritual Toolbox III. Metaphysics IV. Title

Library of Congress Catalog Card Number: 2013943626

ISBN: 978-1-886940-43-7

Cover Art and Layout: www.noir33.com
Book set in: Times New Roman, Californian FB
Book Design: Tab Pillar

Published by:

PO Box 754
Huntsville, AR 72740

WWW.OZARKMT.COM
Printed in the United States of America

ST. MARY PARISH LIBRARY
FRANKLIN, LOUISIANA

# Acknowledgements

**My Guides (GG)—Without Jeremy, Gilbert, Olexeoporath, Akhnanda, Charles, and Selena, there would be no books or weekly Facebook messages from the GG.** Thank you for pushing me forward and always being nearby—especially as I took those first scary steps out of the "spiritual closet." I am eternally grateful for your continued love and guidance.

**Sunna Rasch**—my dear friend and mentor, who so recently passed over to the other side. On this side of the veil, she gave me the courage to pursue metaphysics and writing. From that side of the veil, she carefully explained important information about our Higher Selves for this book. Thank you for your continued encouragement and friendship.

My mother & grandmother: **Marjorie Knapp Ihburg** and **Marjorie Knapp**: Both are on the other side, yet I feel their fabulous, supportive, positive energy every day of my life. Thank you for always being with me.

My husband, **Ted Dylewski**: Thank you for understanding when I'm late doing things because I need to channel a message, answer emails, and write posts; and thank you for all your love and support through the years. There would be no books without your help. We are very close to enjoying what we've worked so hard to build together, and I can't wait to start our travels. Now… hang in there while I get started on one more book!

**Heidi Winkler**: Thank you for not yelling at me when I forget about (or ignore) the six-hour time difference between us and insist that you go over channeled information with me immediately. And thank you for being such a great friend who is always there for me; now…move back to Orlando! *Please*!?!

**Dolores & Julia Cannon** and the Gang at Ozark Mountain Publishing (especially **Shonda** and **Nancy**): Thank you for your continued support and guidance. A big thank you, also, for putting up with me and answering all my questions. **And a very special thank you to IteRa Clehouse, my editor at Ozark Mountain Publishing, for her insightful suggestions, guidance, and advice. There is no doubt that this is a better book because of IteRa.**

My ***dear friends who took the time to read over the manuscript*** for this book and make it so much better: a huge THANK YOU to **Heidi Winkler, Shelly Wilson, Keri Nola, Mitchell Osborn,** and **Sara** (She's like "Cher!").

**My fellow authors and teachers, who contributed so much to this book**. It would not be a "spiritual toolbox" without your amazing and important contributions:

**Shelly Wilson:** Thank you for allowing me to include your wonderful Honor Our Light, Releasing & Forgiveness, and Quick Chakra Balancing Exercises and Meditation. This book happened because of your incredible and astonishing friendship and support. You are so remarkable that I would need an entire chapter to thank you properly.

**Mitchell Osborn:** Thank you for writing a guest chapter, which is more truly a mini-workshop about the Five Dimensions of Wellness—and so much more than I ever expected, knowing how busy you are. I am so grateful for your kindness and continued friendship and support. Be forewarned that I'm looking to you for future collaborations—you are so crucial to this planet.

**Irene Lucas:** Thank you for writing a guest chapter and sharing the 5 Steps to Creating Unlimited Abundance, Healing, and Health with the very important Lightworkers who are reading this book. An email or chat with you is like being dipped in a delicious vat of positive vibrations. Your work is so essential, and I am in continued awe of you. Thank you for being my friend.

**Paige Hall-Ferraro:** Thank you for writing a guest chapter and especially for sharing so much of yourself and your light as you took the helm to enlighten our readers about choosing, cleansing, and programming crystals, and especially for the powerful crystal meditation you wrote for this book. You are amazing and my appreciation knows no bounds.

**Lori Carter:** Thank you for sharing your expertise about the Akashic Records in my column and this book. What I learned from my Akashic Reading with you led to much insight and understanding about my current lifetime. You have the most incredible energy, and I'm looking forward to working together again.

**Craig Howell:** Thank you for allowing me to use your amazing compositions on the CD that accompanies this book. You are always there cheering me on, providing insight, and, of course, creating the most amazing channeled music I have ever heard in my life. You are dazzling and your music is pure magic. I am so happy to be on this journey with you.

**Sara:** Thank you for your help in understanding *walk-in's* and for opening up the way you did with such personal information. In addition to being such a great friend (what happens when an Arcturian and Sirian walk into a bar?), you are also quite enlightening. A day without an email from you is like a day without sunshine.

**Shirley Battie***:* A huge thank you to my fellow Lightworker, pal, and confidante on this journey for the truth of our existence. Your input on *walk-ins* was essential and so important. The work you've done and are still doing all over the world is so vital. When I grow up, I want to be just like you!

Huge thanks to the very important ***Lightworkers who took the time to share essential information to help our planet***: **Suzanne Miller** of Philadelphia, PA; **Bex Gibbons** of New Zealand; **Vickie Stover-Carlstrom** of Satuma, FL; **Carolyn Duff Laughlin** of Fishers, IN; **Heidi Winkler** of Hawi, HI; **Sara Achor** of Colombus, OH; **Cherie Kiley** of Brockton, MA; **Lisa Crowder** of DuPont, WA; **Shannon Carpenter** of Springdale, AR; **Viki Viertel** of Lakeland, MN; **Jennise Davis** of St. Albans, NY; **Teresa Moris** of Glenhaven, WI; **Sue & John Brennan** of Orlando, FL; **Stacy Herr** of Lancaster, PA; **Chere Menville** of Clearfield, KY. You walk your talk and our planet is a better place because of your kindness and energy.

Special thanks to a very important group of people who are ALWAYS there for me and who keep me thoroughly grounded: My **sisters*:* Kathy Seeley and Debbie Smith**; and my **aunts*:* Janet Collins and Sandra Knapp.**

Heartfelt thanks to all of my fabulous **friends and relatives** for their continued support, for liking my posts, and for making me smile when I read and hear about their adventures.

# Dedication

This book is dedicated to YOU, my fellow sojourners on this soul adventure.

In fact, my Guides have an important message for you:

> ***Know how important and powerful you are. It is because of you that human beings have earned the right to incarnate in 5D energy, and it is because of you that the human race continues to evolve. The things that you consider small are truly monumental as you continue to create positive energy, raise vibrations, and help planet Earth. Your Guides are with you always. Meditate, listen, and hear them.***

# Table of Contents

# INTRODUCTION: MEET THE GG

"Another book? Why do we need to write another book when there are already so many great and important books out there?"

That was my response when my Guides told me it was time to get back to work. I learned during the writing of *Windows of Opportunity* that there is no winning an argument with Spirit, yet once again I continued to argue my point that there was no need for me to write another book. I couldn't imagine what we or someone else had left to say that we hadn't already covered.

They patiently explained to me that this endeavor is meant for a *particular* audience who will put its contents to proper use for the continued evolution of the individual Lightworker, the human race, and our planet.

Oh . . . by the way, the Guide Group ("GG") means 3D Earth, not 5D Earth, but we'll get to that later.

They also tolerantly explained to me that Spirit is continually channeling information and wisdom in diverse ways *and* via multiple instruments of communication in order to reach as many as possible. They said that we are drawn to and absorb information more completely from the authors, channels, and fellow Lightworkers with whom we personally resonate.

I understood their point, yet at the risk of sounding argumentative, I voiced my opinion that perhaps instead of more books, it was time to take what we had already read and absorbed and spend more time putting it into action, so that we could *move ourselves forward* during this segment of our evolution. According to the "GG," I'm not 100% wrong in my thinking—the time to take action ***is*** now, but there's still much more that Spirit has to communicate to us. Why? Because we're ready for it; we are *ready* for ***BIG*** Lightworker explanations at this point in our development because we've earned them. This clarification left me no room for further argument; so I stopped whining, went to my laptop, and got to work.

And now, I'm greatly honored to introduce you to the Guide Group (GG) for *Spiritual Toolbox*:

**Jeremy**

Jeremy was the lead Guide for the GG in *Windows of Opportunity*. He's the Guide that came through when I made first contact with Spirit during an automatic writing class back in the 1980s. He's my main Guide for this lifetime, and he occasionally shares his wisdom and guidance on my Facebook Author page. He is my rock and my "go to" Guide when I need clarification about whatever's happening in my life. He is very down-to-Earth and quite serious when it comes to the importance of the role Lightworkers are playing in the evolution of the human race. To read some of his insights, see http://www.facebook.com/#!/SherriCortlandAuthor.

**Gilbert**

Gilbert channeled much of the information in *Raising our Vibrations for the New Age*. He and I are old pals, and we've teamed up for many projects during many lifetimes together and between incarnations as well. If you've been to my Facebook Author page, you already know that Gilbert is a frequent contributor of messages on GG Fridays and is not shy about utilizing social media to reach out to Lightworkers. Working with Gilbert is a lot of fun—he's funny with a bit of a sarcastic sense of humor, and he pulls no punches.

**Akhnanda**

In *Raising our Vibrations for the New Age*, Akhnanda channeled the galactic information and a couple of meditations to help us raise our vibrations and acclimate to 5D energy. Akhnanda's home base is Arcturus, and I've worked with Akhnanda on many projects through the eons and ethers, as Arcturus is also (so I'm told) my home base. Souls incarnating on planet Earth stop first at Arcturus for assistance acclimating to the lower energies here, so Akhnanda's experience and wisdom regarding transitioning from 3D to 5D energy is invaluable to this project.

## Olexeoporath

If you've read my other books or check the Facebook messages on GG Friday, you've heard of Olexeo. He was the second Guide to come through to me when I first started automatic writing with Spirit, and his energy was so strong that I broke several pencils adjusting to it. Olexeoporath has lent his assistance to the GG in each of my books and, as I recall, he was channeling information about Arcturus back in the 1980s. Interestingly, until this very moment I never asked him where he was from. I think this is because I was so blown away by and in awe of his energy—I wrote down whatever he channeled and asked very few questions. I just asked him about his origin, and here's his reply:

OL: ***Sherri, I am from the Source, as are we all, but I have spent much time on Arcturus and also in the Pleiades and Sirius. My part in this group is to help you understand that we are all connected to each other and to the Source.***

And there you have it. In my experience, Olexeoporath has always been a Guide who does *not* waste words.

## Selena

Selena was the third Guide to write with me through automatic writing. She worked with me for about three months in 1988, and I heard from her only rarely until I started GG Fridays on my Facebook page where she is a frequent contributor of messages. I remember feeling when I first met her that her energy was so different from Jeremy and Olexeoporath—much gentler, yet firm and commanding. Again, because I was so new at channeling when we first worked together, I didn't ask her a lot of questions, so I will rectify that right now.

SC: Selena, thank you for being part of this group. Will you share with us where you're from and your role in this group?

Sel: ***Sherri, I am here because I am a master of advanced energy levels, and I will share with you meditations that will assist Lightworkers in adjusting and balancing their energies as they continue to evolve. When I worked with you before, it was to***

***adjust your energy so you would be able to receive information from Spirit without becoming depleted.***

SC: Thank you. Will you share with us where you're from?

Sel: ***I am from the Source, as are you, as are all souls. Sherri, I am part of many universes and have spent time working with many planets in many systems and dimensions. I am an inter-dimensional energy expert, and I go wherever I am needed. Like dwelling on past lives, it makes no sense to dwell on other planets where you may have lived a lifetime or 100 lifetimes; what is important for you now is to understand our connection to the Source and to continue to move forward as spiritual beings. This is why we are writing this book.***

SC: Thank you, Selena.

**Sunna**

If you read *Windows* and/or *Vibrations*, the name Sunna Rasch will be familiar to you. She founded Periwinkle National Theatre for Young Audiences, the company that produced many important human growth plays, including the one I mentioned in *Windows* to help kids deal with bullies. While on planet Earth, she was always way ahead of her time, and prior to passing over in the summer of 2011, she had been my close friend and mentor for twenty-five years. In fact, we took psychic development classes together, and she was sitting right next to me on the night I made *first contact* with Jeremy during a workshop about automatic writing. During another workshop about reincarnation, we were told that she had been my mother in a previous life, which made perfect sense to us because we argued like we were related! When she passed over, I hoped for a message from her, and I got so much more. She is part of this GG, and I am honored to share her wisdom and guidance in these pages.

I'm actually laughing out loud right now because these introductions feel like I'm listing a cast of characters in a playbill, which I'm sure is Sunna's influence since she was, after all, a playwright and producer during her previous incarnation with us. And now that you've met the gang and know who is responsible for the channeled information in this book, let's look at what they intend to accomplish.

SC: Hi everyone, will you please share with us what you intend to accomplish with this book—particularly what you want us to get out of it?

GG: ***Dear readers, it is our intention to give you information that may surprise and delight you to the point where you will shake your heads and say, "Oh yes, this makes so much sense; I'm so happy to remember this now. It will make my life easier going forward."***

***We say this because all that we will speak of is not new information. You know all of this already, and as the veil continues to thin and your vibrations continue to rise, we are able to bring you more and more information that you can put to good use as you face the trials and tribulations of life as an evolving human being.***

***We may also speak of things that will cause you to shake your head and say, "No, this cannot be true."***

***But you have earned the right to move to the next level; you are ready for this information. You have been on Earth long enough, you have read and assimilated the information in many books containing important wisdom, and you have met enough fellow Lightworkers to know that you are important. Extremely important! The continued evolution of this planet is dependent upon you, and the time is now for you to know exactly who you are and how you are connected to the Source that most call God. Your work is not done, and it is time for you to fully realize your power and abilities. It is time for direct communication with Spirit for all, not for just a few. All are capable of direct communication.***

SC: Thank you. What I'm also getting from you is that you want us to turn our best intentions into actions and our actions into habits in order to help ourselves, each other, and our planet. Am I getting this correctly?

GG: ***Yes. That is correct. Intentions are important, and they get the universal ball rolling, so to speak, but taking that next step from intention to action is what allows Lightworkers to move forward. Read, question, and digest all the information you can, determine what you want to do, use your thoughts and words to articulate your intentions, and then follow through with action. That is your collective challenge as Lightworkers.***

SC: Thank you.

══✦══

We've got a lot to cover, so let's get started!

# SECTION ONE

# WHO ARE WE?

# Chapter One: We Are God

Roll up your sleeves because we're getting right to the point. The GG is wasting no time getting to the core of what they want to get across in this book.

GG: ***Sherri, the information we bring to you and your readers today is such that it may seem difficult to believe or comprehend. It may perhaps appear blasphemous to some, especially to one such as yourself who has carried over residual fear from a past life. What we share now, we share from a place of love and a desire for Lightworkers to have a more complete understanding of the workings of our souls in order to know who you really are.***

***We are, each of us, a spark of the Creator, a spark of the Source, a spark of what many refer to as God; the name does not matter. It is understanding who we are that matters. We are part of the Source/Creator/God. As human beings, we are blind to this knowledge and feel separated while in body on planet Earth. Nevertheless, we are made up of the same cosmic stuff, the same material as the God entity. We are very much part of God, and for the remainder of our conversations on this subject, we will use the term "Source," but you can interchange it with Creator or God, if you like. They are the same entity.***

═✦═

I'm going to jump in here for just a moment. It's a fact that I carry a great deal of residual fear regarding writing about anything deemed to be non-Christian, and it's because I was burned at the stake as a heretic in the 1500s. It's very difficult for a soul to recover from something like that, and this residual fear is sometimes overwhelming for me. I believe that it's the source of my on-going struggle with publishing what the GG channels to me.

That *heretical* lifetime is the reason why I initially had to be dragged kicking and screaming out of the New Age or "spiritual closet." It's why I didn't want to include the information about Judas in *Windows of Opportunity* or write about the fact that there's no such place as "hell" in *Vibrations*. When I included the channeled information bites about organized religion *not* existing on New Earth (which my Guides now refer to as 5D Earth) and that we would understand that the "Creator is not hands-on" in *Vibrations*, I confess that I was afraid. I was afraid of upsetting people, and to be perfectly honest with you, deep down, I was afraid of dealing with whatever *this* century's version of being burned alive at the stake would bring my way.

I thought I was fully out of the closet as I sat down to work with the GG on this book, but I found that I was wrong. As much as I've tried to avoid taking them, it seems that my final steps toward standing tall in my *personal* truth are happening right now, so here goes. I was raised Christian, but I am no longer Christian. I do not believe in organized religion because in my experience, it creates and fosters an "us against them" attitude that I don't think is productive for spiritual growth. I believe that organized religion often limits us spiritually because if we don't believe what our church believes, we might well be ostracized or *gasp!* excommunicated, which is not as bad as being burned at the stake. However, if your friends and your life are tied to a particular church, getting kicked out or being ridiculed for your beliefs can feel a little bit *like* being burned at the stake.

I have a friend whom I love and respect very much who felt she needed to ask her priest for permission to read one of my books—he gave it to her, so evolution *is* taking place. I have other friends whom I also love and respect who won't dare touch one of my books because they think what I write about is anti-God. I'm not anti-God; I'm simply pro-truth. I want to know the truth about our existence. I want to know the truth about God.

I'm not saying here that folks should leave their churches and stop participating in religious activities. What I believe and what I'm saying here is that we shouldn't let religion or any man, woman, or group interfere with our spiritual growth and evolution. Nearly three decades ago, I reached out to Spirit, and I made an unswerving effort to connect with Spirit *directly* because I was on a search for the truth about our existence. I didn't want to wait to read what someone else was receiving—I wanted to receive information and wisdom first-hand. Part of my personal mission for this incarnation is to help others learn how to communicate directly with Spirit, and so I began automatic writing, channeling information from Spirit, and writing the books that have now led me to this volume and this page. And I don't mind sharing with you that I'm scared, very scared, to come this far out of the closet. But fear is something all Lightworkers must face, and so with this book, I am facing my greatest fear of all—sharing what I've received about who we are and how the *system* works. Back to the GG:

GG: ***It is important to understand that we are not separated from the Source; we are very much part of it. Not remembering who we are is part of life on 3D Earth, yet those who are incarnated there experience and learn and send that information back to the Source. We are of the Source, and we have experiences and seek information on behalf of the Origin/Source Entity. The human race is evolving and the knowledge of our true connection to the Source is now making its way to Lightworkers via many channels.***

***Why now? Because you have earned the right to know. You are incarnated in a difficult, dense energy where you remember very little, if anything, of who you are and why you are here. You work and struggle to learn tiny tidbits of truth; you make progress, and your vibration and energy levels increase daily. The desire to know your origin is great, and your energy frequencies have risen to the point that you are able to accept and process this information.***

Celebration is in order. We have made progress to the point where information previously withheld from us because our vibrational level was not yet high enough to handle or process such information during this incarnation is now being made available to us. This is a huge thing! It can also be unsettling to learn that things are not the way we've always believed them to be, especially when it comes to God and religion.

We are part of the Source, meaning that we are part of God. We've all heard this before, but we've skirted around the periphery of what this really means. It means that we are creators just as God is the Creator. What do we create? Well, to start with, we create and bring to fruition our own carefully made plans for learning and growth here on Earth. The big news here though is that we aren't involved in this learning, this human experience, purely for the purpose of the growth of our souls. We create learning opportunities, and we choose to have particular experiences in order to relay new information back to the main entity, back to the Source.

Our souls are much like nerve endings for the Source, seeing and feeling and experiencing life so that we can feed what we learn and experience back to what is essentially the ultimate *home base for our souls*. This information was very disconcerting for me when I first received it, and I immediately called my friend, Heidi Winkler, to discuss and dissect everything that was channeled by the GG on this subject. She doesn't live down the street from me anymore; she now lives in Hawi, Hawaii, which means there is a 6-hour time difference between us, *but I didn't care*. I needed to talk this information through, and being the great friend that she is, she answered her phone at 4:00 a.m. Hawaii time and didn't yell at me. We spent about two hours going over what was channeled, and I realized that it was my ego that didn't want to acknowledge this new information.

My ego didn't like learning that rather than being an independent entity, I am just a tiny part of a much larger entity. My ego didn't want to accept that everything I do during this lifetime is for the purpose of gathering information for someone or something else—namely, the Source. I didn't want to be a nerve synapse; I wanted to be Sherri Cortland. The call to Heidi helped, but it took several more days for me to come to terms with the fact that as I gather information for the Source, I am also gathering information for me because I'm part of the Source. Ai yi yi! This new info was hard for me to come to terms with, and my ego was not being cooperative in the least.

The ego is and has always been so necessary to our survival as we live our lives on planet Earth, but it is also the biggest block to our spiritual growth. Our ego represents our beliefs, our likes and dislikes, and it can be very judgmental. Our ego represents a lifetime of growing and learning, a lifetime of hard work on our part. As we raise our vibrations, part of our evolutionary process is breaking free of our ego—something so important to us that we've personally crafted it over a lifetime. But breaking free of the hold our ego has on us is a **must** for spiritual growth, and this is because at the heart of our spiritual growth is the understanding or the *awareness* of who we really are. In order to achieve this awareness, we must unlock the handcuffs that keep us bound to the belief that what we are physically in this incarnation is **all** that we are. Moving past our ego is the key to unlocking these handcuffs.

We have no choice: in order to move forward, we must wrestle with and subjugate our ego so that we can break free of its shackles. Once we accomplish this, we will realize and accept who we really are. We are God. We are the Source. We are Creators in our own right, and according to the GG, this awareness leads to important new information:

GG: ***With awareness comes the knowledge that the Source is not hands-on, and everything that happens to you is because you planned it. When your life does not go according to plan, it is because of freewill on your part or because you or another incarnated being had a short circuit, which affected your original plan. With this knowledge comes the understanding that we are personally responsible for our lives. This knowledge is evolution, not blasphemy.***

==✦==

What the GG say about our lives not going according to plan because of freewill or because we or someone else do/does something to upset our carefully laid plans is a key point when it comes to the awareness of who we are.

According to the GG, rape, murder and suicide are not planned events; they are events that are caused by short circuits in the brain of a human being. These short circuits happen when someone takes on too much for one lifetime or when a soul is abused or forced to experience awful things, especially at a very young age. No one sets out to be a murderer and no spiritual guide would ever condone such a thing or allow it to be incorporated in someone's life plan. No one sits at the planning table carefully constructing windows of opportunity that contain rape, murder, or suicide. Yet these things happen. The next level of awareness that comes with this knowledge is pretty big, too; according to the GG, there is no such thing as evil.

GG: ***When things go wrong, they go wrong because of the ego, not because a soul is evil. It is crucial to spiritual growth to understand that the ego is not who you really are. The ego is shaped by your experiences as human beings, and part of being aware is to question the conclusions that the ego places before you. In order to make decisions that allow higher levels of awareness and expedite spiritual growth, a thorough examination of the conclusions, judgments and calls to action initiated by the ego must take place.***

══✦══

As we come to the awareness that no soul is evil—and how could it be when it is a piece of God—the next step is the realization that there is no heaven and there is no hell. These *places* of reward and punishment are fabrications created by man to exert control over the masses.

When I was writing *Raising Our Vibrations*, the GG for that book dictated that if souls fervently believed in heaven and hell, they would find what they so zealously believed in when they initially crossed over but would eventually move on and get back into the business of the fourth dimension. The dictation on the subject of hell prompted me to do some research, which I present to you again in abbreviated form because it very much pertains to what the current GG is sharing with us now.

- The word "hell" is not used in approximately two-thirds of the Bible. In fact, the word "Sheol" in the Old Testament is sometimes translated as *hell*, but it actually means *grave. Sheol* is where everyone in the Old Testament went when they died—good or evil, Jew or Gentile.

- The accuracy of word translations in the Bible is something we all need to think about because it's very easy to manipulate a translation to achieve one's personal goals. Unless we read the original text in the original language, how can we know for sure what was actually written?

- During the first Council of Nicaea in 325 AD, Emperor Constantine and a council of Christian bishops made decisions regarding what would be included in Christian doctrine, which books would become part of the Bible, *and* settled the debate regarding the divinity of Jesus Christ. IF these are indeed the things that took place at the Council of Nicaea, is it such a big stretch to entertain the idea that certain subjects (i.e., reincarnation and karma) could have been excluded and the concept of hell added?

- Why add the concept of hell to the Bible? Because it's much easier to get folks to do as they're told if they're afraid of spending eternity in a fiery pit if they don't follow the rules/laws set forth by the church.

- Why didn't God mention hell in the beginning of the Bible? According to the Bible, God said the penalty for eating from the Tree of Knowledge of Good and Evil was death—not "eternal life" in fire and brimstone.

- Why weren't Cain, or Sodom and Gomorrah, or any of those who committed the earliest recorded sins warned about hell so they could avoid the sins that would send them there?

- Why didn't Moses include a warning about hell as punishment for breaking the Ten Commandments? Shouldn't such rules come with at least *an idea* of what the punishment would be for breaking them?

And now that we're evolving and gaining a greater sense of awareness about who we are—we *know* that we are part of God—so why, *please tell me why* God would punish Himself? If God sends a soul to a place called *hell*, and we are all sparks of God, pieces of God, doesn't logic dictate that God would be sending Himself to hell? This makes no sense at all.

My Guides channel that there is no heaven and there is no hell—only learning and experiences. That is why we are here—to learn, to experience. It's no surprise to anyone reading this book that planet Earth is a schoolhouse, and so, too, are other planets, and dimensions and timelines. The entire multiverse is a schoolhouse, but it's also a communications network that feeds information back to the Source.

The GG is also making a point here about *personal responsibility*, which is something that I've been writing and lecturing about since 2009. Windows of opportunity and relationship villains are tools that we've included in our life plans to help us recognize what's going on in our lives and figure out what we came here to learn and experience. In Chapters Eleven, Twelve, and Thirteen, we'll quickly review these concepts found in my last two books, and rather than simply reading about them, this time we'll have what amounts to a mini-workshop and start putting these tools to work for us *today*, so we can immediately expedite our spiritual growth. Let's end this chapter with a few more words from the GG.

GG: ***Something important that Lightworkers have forgotten is that we are all upper level beings who are merely expressing ourselves as beings on different planets and in different dimensions to allow us to learn new things, grow as we wish to grow, and for those still involved in karma, to fulfill their karmic debts. We are so much more than what we think we are. We are very much part of the Source, made of the same stuff as God, and we are only "separated" from the Source in this way because it is necessary for us to accomplish specific goals. It makes no sense to be awake if being awake inhibits us from having a specific experience. This is also why we should not judge each other.***

***We are all plodding on, plodding ahead, and making the most we can of our incarnations. To judge is to waste time when there is so much work we have to do on ourselves and for ourselves. There is so much talk and focus about becoming fifth-dimensional beings, but truly, many souls presently incarnated are already fifth-dimensional beings and beyond.***

We human beings do have a tendency to judge each other, and the one person we tend to judge most harshly is ourselves. Learning to forgive ourselves is crucial to moving forward, and this is a lesson that I've been working on personally for quite a while. Chapter Thirteen with its reminder about relationship villains includes exercises to help us spot them in our lives, but what about the times that *we* act as relationship villains for other people? When we look back at things we've done in the past, were we doing those people a spiritual favor, or were we just being mean? It's hard to tell while we're in body, but two things come to mind:

1. If we can reach out to those we feel we have wronged and apologize, it may well give both parties closure; and

2. If we can't find the person in order to apologize, then we can send an apology through our Guides.

We can ask our Guides to speak to the Guides of the person we feel we've *wronged* and ask them to relay our apologies. I realize that the person receiving the apology will only know about it on a soul level, not on a conscious level, but *we will have taken action.* That action will help us move forward because forgiving ourselves is crucial to our progress; recognizing how our own behavior affects others and forgiving ourselves are crucial to expediting our spiritual growth.

One of my close friends, author, Reiki Master and Intuitive Medium, Shelly Wilson (www.Shellyrwilson.com), includes exercises in her workshops that focus on honoring who we are and forgiving ourselves. I asked Shelly for permission to include them in this section, and she kindly agreed. This book isn't called *Spiritual Toolbox* for nothing! We have *lots* of exercises coming up; the two that follow are only the beginning. The GG likes to say that this book is about "putting on our **BIG** Lightworker pants" and taking responsibility for ourselves as we forge ahead. My feeling is that by taking an in-depth look at ourselves, we will absolutely move closer to taking control of our lives and expediting our spiritual growth.

Our first two quick and effective exercises to put the information we've talked about in this chapter into action are from Shelly, and they are both included on the CD accompanying this book.

## Honor Our Light Exercise by Shelly Wilson

This exercise allows us to honor our Light within and ground it into Mother Earth energy.

- Close your eyes.
- Breathe in deeply and exhale anyone and anything that no longer serves you or your higher purpose.
- Envision tree roots coming up through your feet and a vine wrapping itself around your legs. This vine is extending upwards into your root chakra, moving up into your sacral chakra, moving up and extending into your solar plexus chakra, and then into your heart chakra where it rests and grounds you into Mother Earth.
- Now envision white light coming in through your crown chakra.
- Allow the light to move down into your third eye chakra.
- Now watch it move into your throat chakra.
- The light next moves into your heart chakra where it combines with the Mother Earth energy.
- You are now grounded to Mother Earth and to Light.
- Repeat the following mantra three times: I honor the Light within me.
- Now breathe in deeply and exhale.

## Shelly Wilson's Releasing and Forgiveness Advice

This advice from Shelly about releasing and forgiving is followed by a releasing and forgiveness exercise.

*As human beings, we tend to replay scenarios over and over again in our minds, continually asking ourselves, 'What could I have done differently?' or 'What if . . . ?' We also play the 'Should I?' game and worry, 'I should have done this,' or 'I should have done that.' Then this would not have happened.*

*How can you be so sure that what we did wasn't the right thing to do in the bigger universal picture? We may not know for sure, but we do know that we do things for which we seek forgiveness and release. In reality, the decisions we make are because we have free will. Each one of us is having a human experience because we choose to, and learning from our experiences and not repeating them is one of the benefits of being aware.*

*We have the power to forgive ourselves just as we can forgive others. Rather than admonishing ourselves for decisions we've made and then regret, rather than allowing such experiences to define us and weigh us down, we can release ourselves from the pain, heartache, and frustration we hold onto. Now is the time to release and let it go. The past is in the past. It cannot be changed. Allow yourself to let go, so that you can begin anew. New beginnings start with the releasing of old thoughts, and this exercise will assist you in letting go of the past so you can move forward.*

**Releasing & Forgiveness Exercise by Shelly Wilson**

Sit up with your back straight and your palms open to receiving the light energy from the universe.

- Close your eyes.
- Take a few moments to just BE.
- Allow the memory of an experience or individual that you have labeled "unpleasant" to come into your consciousness.
- Do not re-live the experience or try to remember the details. Simply allow this individual, event, or experience to come into your mind.

- Next, acknowledge and release this memory you have labeled "unpleasant" by saying aloud, "I acknowledge. I release."
- Breathe in deeply, and as you exhale, visualize yourself exhaling this experience or individual.
- Continue to allow memories of an experience or individual that you have labeled unpleasant to come into your mind and release them in the same way.

**Note from Shelly**: *Do not try to remember the details of these memories. Simply acknowledge and release them. Breathe in deeply and visualize yourself exhaling the experience or individual.*

Thank you, Shelly! Wow, we've covered a lot so far, and we're going to wrap up this chapter with some insight from GG member Sunna Rasch, my dear friend and mentor who passed over in 2011.

SR: ***Sherri, its Sunna. I'm here with you, Sweetie. There are things that people will like and things that will scare them as evolution and growth continues, but something that must be talked about is that we are all upper level beings who are merely expressing ourselves as people on different planets and in different dimensions to allow us to learn new things, grow as we wish to grow, and for those still involved in karma, to fulfill karmic debts.***

***What is shiny and new about what's happened on Earth is that an entire species has earned the right to incarnate at the fifth-dimensional level, and a fifth-dimensional Earth has been created to accommodate them.***

SC: Um. Hmm. Excuse me, dear Guides, but did I channel that correctly? Did Sunna just say that 5D Earth already exists and . . . the Lightworker Brigade is still *here* on 3-D Earth?

My dear readers, we will address *this* subject in the next chapter.

# Chapter Two: Why Haven't We Transitioned?

Are you wondering why you're still here on 3D Earth? Did you expect to be on 5D Earth by December 2012 at the latest? Well, you're *not* alone, and you're in good company, too. Many channels were given information about transitioning to 5D Earth, and since 5D Earth ***is*** in place, *I* want to know, and I'm sure *you* want to know—what the heck happened? I asked the GG to please explain to us what's going on, and what follows is the transcript of the automatic writing session where I questioned the GG about this subject.

SC: Why haven't all the Lightworkers of the world transitioned to 5D Earth?

GG: ***In time, you will cease this incarnation on third-dimensional Earth, and it will be in a way that will bring closure to the life you've lived and to those in your life; you will not simply disappear. There will be continuity and a passing over, a transitioning to the Other Side.***

SC: In *Vibrations*, you talked about transitioning to 5D Earth and said that many of us would do that. Has something changed?

GG: ***No, nothing has changed. There will simply continue to be a third-dimensional aspect of your Higher Self (you) that will stay put and finish the incarnation at hand. Your soul, your Higher Self, is able to split into many, many versions or aspects of itself and may well have aspects of itself incarnated on both 3D and 5D Earth right now, as well as on many other planets or dimensions.***

SC: So what you're saying is that we've done all this work, raised our vibrations, raised the vibrations of the planet, made it possible for humankind to exist in 5D energy, and we're stuck here?

GG: ***No, Sherri. We're saying that we can't have hundreds of thousands of people simply disappear from the face of 3D Earth. There are many of you who are visiting 5D Earth during your***

***sleep; you just don't recall it because such recollections would interfere with completing this incarnation. There cannot be a gaping hole in the carefully laid life plans of millions of people, and that's what would happen if Lightworkers transitioned en masse. Many, many Lightworkers have left their bodies, and their bodies are now being utilized by walk-ins (See Chapter 9 for more about walk-ins). Others agreed to stay and finish their current incarnation because it affords them the ability to continue to learn and grow, and to do what is considered to be extremely important work on 3D Earth. Others who are incarnated planned to remain here for this incarnation from the beginning of the planning stages for this current lifetime. This is a good time to communicate to your readers that concentrating on the here and now is what will benefit them, the human race, and the planet the most at this time.***

SC: It's kind of disappointing, I think, to know that we're not going to see 5D Earth.

GG: ***Sherri, that is 3D thinking. Who you are now on 3D Earth is only one aspect of your Higher Self. Aspects are not in communication with each other, and so we ask you, "How do you know there isn't an aspect of yourself on 5D Earth right now?"***

***Those of us on this side of the veil applaud the work the Lightworker Brigade has completed and is still doing. You have brought the human species to a new level of being; the human race has evolved, thanks to your efforts. What you've accomplished is a monumental, universal, galactic achievement. But you still have these perfectly good 3D bodies, and there's still work to be done on 3D Earth. What's important now is to continue to make the most of this present incarnation.***

SC: Okay, I'm trying to wrap my head around this. I guess a lot of us pictured a sort of "rapture" type of exodus and thought that we would transition because our energy levels/vibrational levels were raised to a 5D level.

GG: ***Enough people have already increased their energy levels in order for a new fifth-dimensional Earth to be formed, and there are already entities who have transitioned, as we mentioned earlier, leaving their bodies available for walk-ins. When this incarnation***

***is completed, many will choose to reincarnate on 5D Earth, and many will choose other planets and other dimensions—it depends on the goals of their Higher Selves. Transitioning souls (aspects) are reabsorbed by their Higher Selves for a time before continuing their individual path of incarnations and learning. All is as it should be. Thanks to Lightworkers and Starseeds, there has been a continual moving forward when it comes to the evolution of the human race. A mass transitioning with bodies simply disappearing would cause unnecessary chaos, and it makes no sense to waste all of those adult bodies when other souls could make great use of them.***

SC: So what, exactly, then, is the mission of a Lightworker *now*?

GG: ***Sherri, the fact is that there is so much happening on 3rd dimensional Earth at the present time that indicates continued progress. The third-dimensional Earth has its place and is very important because it provides learning opportunities that cannot be found elsewhere. But that does not mean that it can't be improved, and that is why we are working on this book with you. We are asking everyone to continue to raise their vibrations and work towards making 3D Earth a brighter light.***

***There are many things to work on.***

- ***For instance, there can be equality for all races and genders on 3D Earth;***

- ***It can still be a place for souls to work out their karma;***

- ***3D Earth can be a kinder, friendlier, planet for people of differing points of view; and***

- ***Working on finding and utilizing cleaner forms of energy will not affect the usefulness of this planet as a place to learn and grow.***

***We think you get our point, and we're confident that you can think of many more things that can be improved upon as 3D Earth continues to remain an important and viable option for certain types of learning and growth.***

SC: Thank you for this clarification.

GG: ***Go in peace.***

Are you disappointed? I was, *at first*. Well, maybe not just at first, I was pretty upset about this information for several months. But after much meditating on it, I understand the GG's point that millions of people could not simply disappear from the surface of the planet. Knowing how hard it is to live through childhood, why waste perfectly good adult bodies? It makes sense to allow souls to transition and for other souls to utilize the bodies of those who transitioned and don't need them anymore. We'll get into the subject of *walk-ins* in detail in Chapter Nine, but what's striking to me at this moment is the knowledge that those who transitioned did not immediately re-appear on 5D Earth; they were reunited with their Higher Selves first.

# Chapter Three: Our Higher Self

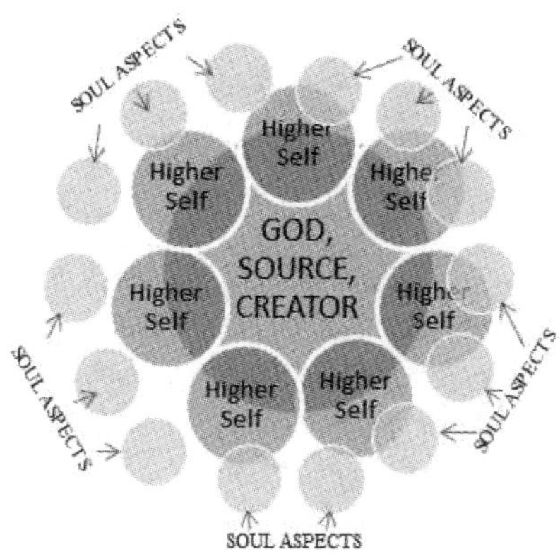


I asked the GG to address the subject of our Higher Self in more depth because of the comments they made about our Higher Selves being able to do the following:

- split into multiple aspects and
- have multiple incarnations simultaneously.

Sunna came through to chat about this subject, and what follows is the transcript from that session.

SR: ***When you pass over, you become one again with your Higher Self, and all that you've experienced and learned is absorbed by your parent being—what is commonly referred to as the Higher Self. The Higher Self passes the information you've brought home on to the Source. The same will happen in the fifth-dimension. It doesn't matter what planet or dimension you're incarnated in. When you finish your incarnation, you go home, and eventually you are reunited with your Higher Self for a time.***

***Something that is important for all to know is that our Higher Selves have many expressions or aspects of themselves running***

***around—and not necessarily all in the same dimension or even the same planet. The Higher Self sends out tentacles, so to speak, to many places in order to learn and grow. The expression of Sherri and the expression of Sunna are one of many expressions from our Higher Selves. We are not really Sherri and Sunna. They are merely roles that we play or, in my case, played in order to learn and grow.***

SC: I've heard this many times before about the possibility of multiple aspects, but if we're re-absorbed, how is it that I'm speaking to my friend Sunna right now?

SR: ***This is where the ego comes in and gives us so much trouble. As an aspect of our Higher Self, we create an individual persona and thoroughly immerse ourselves in who we are for that lifetime. It has to be that way for purposes of learning, experiences, and growth. But we are so much more than the role we are currently playing, for each soul/aspect is a piece of your Higher Self, and your Higher Self is an aspect/piece of the Source. To answer your question, Sherri, I'm speaking to you now as Sunna because that's how you know me, but I am not Sunna—my soul, the aspect that I am, is the sum total of all the roles I've played in countless incarnations on many planets, and further, I'm a part of my Higher Self; therefore, I'm also part of the Source. Do you understand?***

SC: I think I'm getting it. So my soul is currently playing the role of Sherri Cortland, but it's also played a lot of other roles throughout time because of the process of reincarnation. I've played countless roles as an aspect or emissary of my Higher Self, and in so doing, I must have amassed a lot of different skills during those lifetimes. Where are those skills during this lifetime? Wouldn't it make this incarnation easier to access them?

SR: ***Good question, but you're forgetting that you've written a very specific life plan and created windows of opportunity to work on and experience particular things. Remembering and utilizing skills from past lives may hinder the learning experiences of this lifetime. Your lessons would come too easily, or you might gravitate to what is easy for you instead of working on new stuff. This would defeat the purpose of the current incarnation.***

SC: Thank you, Sunna.

═✦═

Our Higher Self is the part of us that connects directly with the Source/God/ Creator. Our Higher Self is the initial spark directly from God, and our soul is a smaller spark of God that originates from our Higher Self. From a business perspective, it's kind of like the hierarchy in a corporation. As individual souls, we report to our Higher Self, and our Higher Self reports directly to Source. Why are we reporting our experiences and learning? Because the Source wants to know all there is to know, all that can be known. Our soul is on a spiritual quest to obtain knowledge for the Source, and the Higher Self is the guiding light for our soul.

Our Higher Self, therefore, transcends our conscious and unconscious mind. In order to **consciously connect and communicate with our Higher Self, we have to move past the ego.** Step one is awareness that our ego is not who we really are. Remember that our ego, which is our conscious mind, is only a small part of who we are. It's shaped by what happened to us as children, what we were told and learned as children, and by all the positive and negative experiences we've had during our current lives. The ego is the representation, the sum total of all we've learned and experienced; however, it's more of a *cover identity*, so we **can** move past our ego.

As we become aware of what our ego is, this awareness allows us to move forward and hear and listen to our Higher Self, who speaks to us 24/7. We already know our Higher Self; it's that "little voice within" that speaks to us from our gut. A "gut feeling" is our Higher Self acting as an internal GPS system, guiding us so we can make better choices for ourselves. Listening to our gut is the same as listening to our Higher Self, which again, leads to us making better choices, which leads to spiritual growth, which leads to increased awareness and higher vibrations. There's much to be gained from learning to tune into and communicate with our Higher Self. We'll talk more about this in Section Two, and now we're going to explore the nature of our Higher Self.

## The Nature of Our Higher Self

Do you recall Sunna mentioning that when we pass over, we are *re-absorbed* by our Higher Selves? I have many friends who are mediums and who bring a lot of comfort to people by channeling our loved ones and friends who have passed over. I'm personally in continual communication with two family members who are on the Other Side, not to mention the Guides I work with to write my books. Sunna's assertion that we are *re-absorbed* took me by surprise. I asked for clarification because I didn't quite understand how we can communicate with individual entities on the Other Side of the veil if they've been *re-absorbed* by their Higher Selves. Here's her answer.

SR: ***At the current moment, your soul is playing the role of Sherri Cortland. When you pass over, for a time your soul will eventually become one again with your Higher Self, and all that you've experienced and learned will be absorbed by your parent being. As an individual soul, you will eventually continue on your own path doing projects, attending classes, being part of focus groups, etc. The role you played as Sherri will be a permanent part of your soul, and the entire lifetime will be recorded in the Akashic Records. It is also recorded in layers of your aura.***

***When someone wishes to speak to a departed loved one—let's use me as an example since I recently passed over—if the soul has not reincarnated, the soul that was Sunna will speak. Once I reincarnate, my Higher Self will be able to speak as Sunna because my Higher Self is as much Sunna as my soul was Sunna. All the information from my lifetime as Sunna was absorbed by my Higher Self when I re-connected to it.***

***Sherri, your hesitation to accept this is nothing more than a reflection of your ego. You don't want to let go of who you are. Once a spark of the Higher Self plays a particular role, a completed individual lifetime becomes part of universally recorded history, and the Higher Self can recall that lifetime and bring forth that particular personality at any time. Your Guides are part of your Higher Self.***

This is new information for me. I've been reflecting on these tidbits for months now, and while I resisted it at first, it does make sense that our Guides are part of our Higher Self. Our Higher Self is the most connected to the Source, and it sends out souls/aspects to create experiences that will ultimately be communicated to the Source. Since the soul develops a plan for an individual incarnation, it makes sense that the Higher Self will want to keep that soul on the right path so that its goals for knowledge are met. As I write this chapter, I think that a small part of me still resists this information just a little bit because I want to hang onto being Sherri Cortland. The lesson here is the realization and acceptance that who we are during this lifetime will always be part of us, but we're *so much more*.

Do not think for one moment that I'm going to let the part about our Guides being aspects of our Higher Self just sit there on the page. Does our Higher Self have aspects that are smarter than we are? Is that why they act as Guides? These are the questions I posed to the GG.

GG: ***No, Sherri. That's not how it is. Each soul reincarnates in the pursuit of knowledge. Therefore, each soul travels on its own journey, experiences different things during different lifetimes, and acquires specific and individual knowledge that makes each soul unique. Some souls never or rarely incarnate; instead, they acquire knowledge through something akin to study programs. As one soul decides to embark on an incarnation—let's say on planet Earth—other souls that are part of that soul's Higher Self will agree to act as Guides, either for the entire length of the incarnation or for different parts of it, depending on the need. The souls acting as Guides for that individual soul will not be incarnated at the same time. Sometimes you have Guides, and sometimes you are a Guide for another aspect of your Higher Self.***

Okay, a lot to process, but the GG delivered this information in a way that I could immediately understand and accept. I had one more question though: "Do we retain the knowledge of our past lives?" I'm aware of past lives that I've experienced, and I know lots of people who know about their past lives, so I wondered how this fit into the picture.

GG: ***Yes, Sherri, you are quite right. Each soul retains the knowledge of its past lives. We draw on our past lives when planning future lives in order to learn lessons based on past experiences, which is what we call "karma." We also plan experiences where we intend to create positive energy; usually this is in situations similar to ones where we've created negative energy during past lives—this would also fall under what we know as "karma." We draw on regrets from past lives and try to correct them as well, and we also plan new experiences for growth and for fun because having fun is important, too.***

Okay, lots of new information; let's recap.

- We are a part of our Higher Self, yet we are separate from our Higher Self in that we have many individual lives that we experience as distinct individuals.
- Our Higher Self absorbs all of our experiences and transmits that information to the Source entity.
- Our Higher Self acts as a Guide, and other aspects of our Higher Self act as our Guides.
- Our souls retain our past lifetimes/personalities for future reference, and can call upon them as needed, i.e., when a medium is reaching out to someone's loved one.
- Each incarnation/personality/lifetime is recorded forever in the Akashic Records

We're going to take a look at the Akashic Records and past lives in Chapter Four, but before we move on, let's take a few minutes to absorb what we've learned so far. If you're anything like me, this was a lot, and I do mean **a lot** to take in. Speaking for myself, I found that the more I meditated on this information, the more it made sense.

The information we've been given in this chapter makes it clear that it's time for us to utilize the knowledge we've been busy accumulating during our current incarnation, and that we're very much responsible for what happens to us while we're incarnated. I know that it's oh so much easier to blame other people for what we perceive as bad things happening to us, but to continue with that line of thinking makes learning the truth of who we are and how we plan our lives even harder to assimilate. Awareness equals responsibility, and with this newfound awareness that we've earned through hard work and dedication to our search for the truth, comes the understanding that it's time for us to let go of a lifetime of beliefs. In a way, we have to let go of ourselves, too, as we embrace our spiritual selves and transcend our ego. And as we do this, our vibrations will continue to rise, and we'll continue to evolve. Let's end this chapter with some wisdom from Gilbert.

Gil: ***We know this is very difficult to digest because as human beings, we are ego-driven, but the souls that incarnated on Earth at this time need to understand this:***

***I will use Sherri as an example. Sherri Cortland is NOT the main entity. Sherri Cortland is just one expression of her Higher Self, one of many souls that are part of that Higher Self, many of whom exist on different planes and planets. She is Sherri for this incarnation but will never be Sherri Cortland again. Such is the way of reincarnation. The ego doesn't like this because the ego is 100% Sherri and wants to continue as Sherri.***

***Human beings have worked hard on 3D Earth to raise their vibrational levels—if it wasn't for this hard work, a 5D Earth would not be possible. And all who have worked so hard will share in 5D Earth, if that's what they choose to do on a soul level. The soul makes the decisions for future incarnations, not the ego of the present incarnation. Lightworkers are now seeing the bigger picture, and much is coming through now to help you see the bigger picture.***

# Chapter Four: The Akashic Records & Past Lives

The Akashic Records were mentioned quite a bit in the last chapter, and it's a subject I've been attracted to for a very long time. I believe that accessing the Akashic Records is a great way to get to the bottom of why we do the things we do, why we're afraid of certain things, why we experience chronic health issues, and oh so important to many of us—why we continue to attract the same relationship issues. Accessing these records is like doing research on the history of our soul, and just writing these words has given me spiritual chills.

The purpose of this kind of soul research is to help us make the most of our current incarnation. The Akashic Records are a tool that we can use to expedite our spiritual growth, and that's why I'm devoting space to learning about them in this book.

The Akashic Records are like a universal library because they contain a permanent record of all of our incarnations, including everything that we've said, thought, and done during those incarnations. They are also referred to as the Hall of Records and the Hall of Knowledge. I first learned about the Akashic Records in the mid-1980s when I joined the Association for Research and Enlightenment (ARE) and read the Edgar Cayce books and case files.

Edgar Cayce, one of the most important healers of the 20th century, helped many people with their health issues by going into a self-induced trance state and accessing the Akashic Records to find the root cause of his clients' ailments. According to the ARE, to get to the Hall of Records, Cayce would put himself into the trance state he used for readings. Next he would experience himself as a dot of light out of his body and be almost overwhelmed by an immense sense of loneliness as he—now identified as that dot of light—went through places of darkness and of light and finally made his way into the Hall of Records, which he described as having no walls. I share Cayce's method of getting to the Akashic Records only as an example because experiences like this are different for everyone.

Please understand that there is no right or wrong way to receive information. I don't want you thinking that just because you don't see yourself as a dot of light that you're doing it wrong. Many people go into a dream-like state. For others, it's like remote viewing while some receive a series of pictures in their minds. There is no right or wrong way to access the Akashic Records and receive information.

Until February 2012 when I met Lori Carter of Blissful Awakenings (www.blissfulawakenings.wordpress.com), my most recent sojourn into the Akashic Records was in the early 80s when my Mother and I attended an ARE Akashic Records workshop in New Jersey and learned about a lifetime we had together in Ancient Rome. Lori Carter is a certified Akashic Record Practitioner and a Karuna & Usui Reiki Master whom I originally interviewed for my Examiner.com column. About two weeks later, I sought her out for an Akashic reading. Here's an excerpt of my original interview with Lori.

SC: Lori, can you give my readers an easy-to-understand explanation of what the Akashic Records are and why they're an important tool for spiritual growth?

LC: *Simply stated, the Akashic Records are an energetic record of every soul's journey on Earth for this lifetime as well as past lifetimes. Why is that important? Well, if we are truly spiritual beings having a human experience—which I believe we are—then there must be a reason or reasons we agreed to put on these Earth suits and forget (at least for the time being) our Divine birthright. Wouldn't it be helpful if we could gain access to our reasons for partaking in this charade? The Akashic Records give us the opportunity to check in and see how we are doing on the agenda we set before coming to Earth.*

SC: That kind of information would be invaluable for those of us who want to expedite our spiritual growth, learn our lessons, and pay our karmic debt quickly with less drama and suffering. How does accessing the Akashic Records work?

LC: *The Akashic Records are an opportunity to have a conversation with our soul to see our lives from a higher-level perspective. They are a powerful tool for looking at patterns and lessons in our lives and for getting to the root of a relationship issue that never seems to get resolved. All of the information that comes through the Akashic Records is kind, gentle, and loving. This is true even when the information coming through was hugely traumatic as initially experienced. As such, there is nothing to fear in working with the Akashic Records. The energy and information are always presented in a gentle, loving manner, but the effects of healing and insight can be profound.*

SC: Lori, the main purpose for my books is to help folks figure out what they're here to accomplish—and to figure it out sooner rather than later. Many of us have *life scripts* where we attract the same type of person into our lives or create similar situations over and over again. If I understand what you're saying correctly, accessing the Akashic Records is a great tool to help us understand the underlying reasons we create life scripts for ourselves?

LC: *Absolutely Sherri. In fact, in my opinion, this is the power of the Akashic Records—to help us recognize and change patterns that are keeping us stuck. These patterns can be ancestral, past life or present life. I repeatedly find that no matter what I am dealing with, opening my Akashic Records is a major step on my healing journey. Working in the Akashic Records has helped me to notice those windows of opportunity you talked about earlier and, therefore, expedite my spiritual growth.*

SC: Accessing the Akashic Records seems like a great way to move ahead spiritually. Lori, I know that you personally work with many people to help them access the Akashic Records. Can you share your process with my readers?

LC*: The good news is that we no longer have to go into a trance like Edgar Cayce did. I access the Akashic Records through the Pathway Prayer process taught by Linda Howe at the Center for Akashic Studies. See her website www.lindahowe.com for more information. I read the prayer using the client's current legal name to ensure the appropriate records are opened, and then we have a conversation about the issues the client wishes to explore. Information is presented to me in images, feelings, words, and* *messages that allow me to frame the topics we are discussing into a higher-level perspective for the client.*

*An Akashic Record reading is not a psychic reading where information is downloaded and given to the client. It's more like a counseling session with the benefit of the soul-level perspective to help see the relationship or situation from the perspective of the masters, teachers and loved ones who are our guides in the Records. I find that the conversational format of an Akashic Record reading is more useful in helping the client see that higher level perspective because it gives my clients a true connection with the information and guidance that comes through.*

SC: Thank you, Lori.

Before we continue our discussion of accessing the Akashic Records as a tool for spiritual growth, let's talk a little bit about past lives. Here's the thing about past lives and why we don't come into this world awake to all of our past experiences: we need to focus on the *here and now* (see Chapter Ten) because that's what's most important for our spiritual growth and the evolution of our soul. *If* we remembered all of our past lives—and most of us have had violent, difficult and just plain sad incarnations (I'm thinking again about the one where I was burned at the stake)—we would spend much of our precious time on Earth dwelling on those lives instead of living in the present. I'm sure *I* would anyway.

Living in the moment and being aware of the repercussions our thoughts, words, and actions have on those around us is what propels us forward spiritually *and* allows us to raise our vibratory levels. Being aware of what we do and say every day and focusing on who we are *now* is what will keep us from acquiring additional karmic debt to be paid during this or future lives.

That said, sometimes knowing about the past lives that *directly* affect our present lives is a very good thing; we just have to "put on our **BIG** Lightworker pants" and put what we learn into perspective. For example, if we have an innate fear of something, it's probably connected to a past life experience. Tracing the source of that fear to the past life where it originated will often allow us to do the following:

1. put the residual energy of that past life back into the Akashic Records where it belongs;
2. release and dissipate any residual fear, and
3. free us to move forward with our current spiritual To Do List and mission.

And . . . *should* we find out that we were Cleopatra or Henry VIII in a past life, instead of lauding it over a friend who may have lived the life of a serf or servant during the same time period, we should instead use this information to look for karmic ties and windows of opportunity to expedite our spiritual growth.

My own Guides have been exceedingly stingy when it comes to telling me about past lives, probably because they know I'll dwell on them, but I've gotten a little bit out of information over the years. I also learned about some interesting past lifetimes during the Akashic Record reading I had with Lori Carter. I know that I've lived several lives in Atlantis, Lemuria and Egypt where I worked extensively with crystals—not just for healing but also for the purposes of helping people acquire knowledge. These lifetimes explain why I'm so fiercely drawn to crystals and why I've been studying them for the better part of thirty years.

During my Akashic reading, I asked Lori what karma I need to work out with my husband, Ted, so we can "get r done" and just relax and travel when we retire in a few years. She told me that Ted and I don't have any karma to work out and that we came together later in life (we were both in our 40s when we met) to finish a lifetime that we started in the 1920s that was cut short when we died together in a tragic train accident as we were heading west to California. That was *good* news—the "no karma" part—*not* the death by train wreck part! What really hit home though—and this epiphany happened *after* I hung up the phone from that reading—was that it was during the 1920s when women finally got the right to vote. Learning from Lori that I was a woman in the 1920s helps explain why I've been a feminist since I was eleven years old, and why I consider Gloria

Steinem, Bella Abzug, and Marlo Thomas to be great American heroes.

The point of sharing my 1920s life with you now is to highlight the fact that knowing about our past lives *can* help shed light on our current feelings, behaviors, and even our fears. Past life regression, hypnotherapy and Akashic record readings can help us understand ourselves better and often give us the missing information we need to move forward. The GG is adamant, though, in cautioning us that **learning about past lives should never take the place of actively living in the present moment** because what we do in the here and now determines what we'll be experiencing in future lifetimes.

GG: ***Sherri, we caution you to limit your desire to research past lives to those that directly affect your current incarnation and mission. It is easy to get caught up in the 'Who was I?' and 'Isn't it cool that I used be' of past life regressions and the acquired knowledge from such meditations and readings. Keep in the forefront of your mind that balance is called for when researching past lives. Do not allow yourself to get caught up in these things to the extent that you lose sight of what is important—watch what you think, do and say every day because that is how you will raise your vibrations, create positive energy, and create less future karmic debt.***

The Akashic Records are the universal storage area of all our incarnations, and we access them through personal meditation, guided meditations (like the one I had at the ARE workshop) and professional readings (like the one I had with Lori). There are also professional hypnotherapists like Dolores Cannon who can help us connect the dots (see www.ozarkmt.com).

To get the most out of Akashic meditations and readings, it makes sense to have a "knowledge-seeking" plan and to know what your intention(s) is/are for the information you'll receive. This plan includes knowing what questions you want/need to be answered. Here are examples of questions you might want to ask:

- Is there something specific about my current journey/lifetime that will help me expedite my spiritual growth or overcome a fear that I have?
- Why do I live where I live?
- Why am I suffering from specific health problems/issues?
- Why do I continually attract the same type(s) of people into my life?
- What am I here to work on during this incarnation?
- Are there past lives that are affecting my current incarnation?

Why go in with a *knowledge-seeking plan*? Because we've all lived countless lifetimes, and the Hall of Knowledge is huge—picture the New York Public Library and think how difficult it would be to find a particular book without a system in place to find it. So put together a list of questions and then meditate on them and relay them to whomever is reading the records for you—and that *could be* your Higher Self.

At the end of this section is a meditation channeled by Akhnanda and Selena to help you access the Akashic Records. If you are new to accessing the Akashic Records, before you try it, keep a couple things in mind:

- Be patient. If you get nothing the first or second time, don't give up.
- Hypnotherapist and Akashic Records expert, Dr. Bruce Goldberg suggests that beginners start out by focusing on events that they know about, i.e., events that you can research after your meditation so you can compare what you received to what's been written about the event. Do this several times with different events as you hone your skills before moving on to events from your own life. For more information about Dr. Goldberg, see http://www.drbrucegoldberg.com/AkashicRecords.htm

Let's get to that meditation.

Akhnanda and Selena channeled the following meditation exercise to help us access the Akashic Records for the purpose of spiritual growth; you'll also find this meditation included on the CD that accompanies this book. And here's something *really* special: my dear friend, author, artist, channeler, and music composer, Craig Howell has allowed me to include his powerful and ethereal music to accompany the following meditation exercise. In fact, Craig's music is part of every meditation and exercise on the CD that accompanies this book. For further information about Craig, see his website http://www.cdbaby.com/Artist/CraigHowell/.

Before we get to the meditation, here's how this wonderful fusion of channeled material came about. I fell in love with Craig's CD, *Mayan Days of Sound* the first time that I played it, which was in my car driving to work. About five minutes into it, I had to pull over to the side of the road because I realized that I was going into a spontaneous meditative state and might just be leaving my body—*not* cool when you're driving in rush hour traffic on I-4 in Orlando. Listening to this CD, I could feel my vibratory level changing, and it's now my go-to CD when I meditate . . . safely . . . in my chair . . . *at home*. I love this CD so much that I wrote to Craig and asked permission to use some of the selections as background music for all of the guided meditations on the CD accompanying this book, and much to my delight, he agreed to allow me to use his fabulous music. Just make sure that when you plug in the CD, you do it at home and not in your car! As you listen to what Craig has composed, combined with the meditation exercise from Selena and Akhnanda, you'll feel your vibrations begin to rise, and you'll know why I'm so excited about this meditation.

**Meditation Exercise to Access the Akashic Records**

- Sit upright or lay down, whatever is most comfortable for you.
- Close your eyes and breathe deeply.
- Inhale and exhale.
- Inhale and exhale.
- Inhale and exhale.

- Begin to relax each part of your body, beginning with your head.
- Feel your head and neck relaxing as you continue to inhale deeply and exhale deeply.
- Relax the muscles in your face.
- Next relax your arms and hands as you take deep, cleansing, relaxing breath.
- And now your legs and feet.
- Continue breathing in and out as you feel yourself melting into a state of peaceful relaxation.
- Set your intention for this meditation with these words:

I am wrapped in and protected by the light as I seek the truth found in the Akashic Records. Higher Self, I undertake this journey with the highest of intentions; please guide and assist me to comprehend and use the information I receive for the highest good of my soul.

- Continue to relax as you begin to turn your attention inward and visualize your third eye chakra, located on your forehead between your eyebrows.
- Let your attention remain here as you center your attention on your third eye and watch it whirr and spin in a clockwise direction. See the vibrant indigo color of the third eye chakra as you continue to breathe in and out.
- Allow yourself to separate now from the place where you're seated. As you continue to breathe and focus on your third eye chakra, all distractions fade away.
- Breathe.
- Take another breath in and out as you begin to notice a stirring in your third eye chakra as images begin to form there.
- Don't question what you see. Just take notice of what you see and hear as you focus on your third eye chakra.
- Now focus your mind and specifically ask to see an event or ask a question from this lifetime or a past lifetime.

Higher Self, with the purest of intentions for the growth of my soul and the benefit of all involved, I request knowledge from the Akashic Records about (Your Legal Name Here). Here is my question: ------?

- Continue to breathe as you see or hear the requested information imparted to you.

Thank you, Higher Self, for your assistance today. Know that I will use what I have learned for the spiritual growth of my soul.

- Slowly begin to stretch your arms and legs and move your hands and feet. When you feel ready, open your eyes. If you feel disconnected or lightheaded, continue to stretch and ground yourself fully before getting up.

If you want to use crystals to help you access the Hall of Records, go right ahead. I've always used clear quartz, amethyst and moldavite; they make a very potent trio when you work with them at the same time. In *The Crystal Bible, a Definitive Guide to Crystals* by Judy Hall, Judy recommends the following three crystals to facilitate access to the Akashic Records:

**Lepidolite**: Facilitates shamanic and spiritual journeying and helps access the Akashic Records.

**Merlinite:** Facilitates reading the Akashic Records and assists in journeying to past and future lives. Holds the imprint of the combined knowledge of shamans and alchemists. Gives access to the shamanic and spiritual realms.

**Moldavite:** Said to be of extraterrestrial origin. A very high-energy stone helps connect with Higher Self, Ascended Masters and cosmic messengers. Helps facilitate past and future life journeying and downloads Akashic Records, which then have to be processed and made conscious.

# SECTION TWO

# COMMUNICATING WITH SPIRIT

# Chapter Five: Messages Are Great; Conversations Are Better!

The more we pay attention to what's happening around us, the more we will see and hear messages from Spirit. For example, when you get a feeling to turn left when you were planning to turn right, that's a message from Spirit. When you hear the same song over and over, or you see the same number over and over, or you always look at the clock at the same time each day, these occurrences are messages from your Guides, Angels, and sometimes your Higher Self. We call these experiences *synchronicity*. For in-depth information on this subject, visit synchronicity expert Mary Soleil's website www.marysoleil.com and read her remarkable book, *I Can See Clearly Now: How Synchronicity Illuminates Our Lives*. Bottom line—when these things occur, they are messages from Spirit.

Being aware of what's going on around us and recognizing messages that come to us in songs, numbers, and synchronicity is important—and a very big deal—yet these messages are also one-sided communications. What I mean is that we can recognize we're hearing "Last Train to Clarksville" for the 10th time this week, but *what exactly is the message*? If you have conversations directly with Spirit, you can always ask, "Hey, I heard this Monkees' song ten times already, but I'm still not getting it. What's the message here?" In the next sub-sections, we're going to talk about several different ways that we can converse with our Higher Self, Guides, and Angels.

**Visiting a Psychic Medium**

Visiting a psychic medium is one way of contacting Spirit. Even though it's not one-on-one, let's talk a little about this form of communication. A medium is someone who can contact, channel, and receive messages from Spirit, including pets. Thus, mediums help us receive important messages from our loved ones, *and* they give us the comfort of knowing that our loved ones are happy and well on the Other Side of the veil.

I've had readings from psychics since I was eighteen years old, but my first experience with a psychic medium took place around 1996 in Cassadaga, Florida, a town where many psychics and mediums live and work. I met with Birdie, who at the time had an office in the Cassadaga Hotel and now works out of her own place down the street.

As I followed her up the steps to her office, she told me that she was having trouble breathing and asked if I knew anyone who passed over who had lung problems. I couldn't think of anyone. All through our session, Birdie continued to say she was having trouble breathing, and I continued to have no idea what she was talking about until finally after about twenty minutes, she said, "Doris is here."

Well. Then I *knew.* Doris is my ex-mother-in-law, and she died of lung cancer. Her son and I divorced the year before this session took place, and I wasn't around the family when Doris was diagnosed with lung cancer. My ex-husband had told me that no one in the family wanted anything to do with me, and so I stayed away.

Doris had a message for me that was too personal to print here, but thanks to Birdie, I was able to not only receive a message from Doris, but I was also able to say some things to her that I'd wanted to say following my divorce but lost the chance when she passed. Her message to me made a huge difference in my life. I definitely got closure that day, and I'm still in awe of Birdie's ability to communicate with Spirit on behalf of those of us on this side of the veil.

I cried my eyes out the whole time I was in Birdie's office, especially when I got that message from my ex mother-in-law—just like I cry my eyes out every time I watch Lisa Williams (http://www.lisawilliams.com) do her thing on *Lisa Williams, Life Among the Dead.* I remember the first time I saw Lisa Williams on TV. I called my sisters and told them to watch. Then I just cried and cried through the entire show. There's something about the opportunity to speak to our loved ones that makes me emotional beyond belief. I'm crying now just writing this.

Tears aside, I recently started watching *Long Island Medium* with Theresa Caputo, and honestly, I tape it so I can watch it when I'm by myself because just like Lisa Williams, Theresa Caputo makes me weep, weep, weep with happiness when she goes up to someone in the gym or restaurant and gives them a message from Spirit. To be perfectly honest, I *also* like to watch it alone because I'm an ugly crier. To learn more about Theresa, see www.facebook.com/pages/Theresa-Caputo.

When it comes to communicating with Spirit, I'm a big supporter of spending some time with a medium, and I'm lucky to have two medium friends who continually help me grow spiritually and hone my own communication skills. I first met Shelly Wilson at Ozark Mountain Publishing's 2009 Transformation Conference where I was speaking, and she was attending. She's an author and a Reiki Master who realized that her true calling was to be a medium and went on to study with Lisa Williams and James van Praagh—really, how cool is that? To learn more about Shelly and her books, see her website www.shellyrwilson.com/.

The thing I love the most about Shelly is what I also love about my friend, psychic medium Mitchell Osborn. See his website for more information about him (www.intuitivemessenger.org). They don't just act as a conduit; they use their gifts to help their clients learn and grow. From my perspective, that's one of the most important things human beings can do for one another, and Shelly and Mitchell work with their clients to help them become empowered and make confident decisions. My point here is that communicating with Spirit isn't just about receiving messages; it's also about helping us learn to take responsibility for our own decisions and our own progress. Again, I say mediums are great, but unless you have one living with you (and even if you do), it makes sense to learn to communicate *directly* with Spirit, especially your Higher Self, and that's exactly what we're going to concentrate on for the rest of this section.

**Chatting with our Higher Selves in Meditation**

How often do we say or think, "I wish Spirit would speak to me"? Consider that wish granted because Spirit speaks to us every day of our lives. To hear what's being said to us, all we have to do is the following:

- be quiet;
- listen; and
- of course, the most difficult challenge of all—**trust what we hear!**

Every time we have a *gut* feeling about something, that's our Higher Self speaking to us, guiding us on the road to spiritual development and better decisions—just like a GPS guides us when we need driving directions. Becoming aware of our gut feelings is a great way to start listening to our Higher Self, and more importantly, *paying attention* to what our gut tells us goes a long way towards expediting our spiritual growth.

I believe that meditation is the best way to listen to what our Higher Self is communicating to us, and with practice, we get better and better at learning to sit quietly and clearly hear what our gut is saying to us. The more practiced we become at listening, the more likely we are to pay attention to that little voice within (which you know is your Higher Self) as it directs us to make the choices that are better for us in the long run. Therefore, meditation not only allows us to commune and communicate with our Higher Self, it also improves our quality of life and expedites our spiritual growth—even if we only meditate for a few minutes a day.

I started meditating on a daily basis when I was working on a degree in Public Relations at Mt. St. Mary College in Newburgh, New York. One semester I signed up for a class called "Mediation East and West." Well . . . that's what I *thought* I was signing up for. I actually signed up for "Meditation East and West." There was a typo in the course description, and you should have seen my face that first night of class when the sister/nun handed out the syllabus! I *learned* how to meditate because of a "misprint," but I *continue* to meditate decades later because it helps me stay calm, cool, and collected no matter what's going on around me. It also allows me to balance my chakras—something we're going to talk more about in Section Seven. Most importantly, though, it allows me to have on-going daily interaction and communication with my Higher Self.

I promise you that *our little voice within* is much easier to hear and listen to when we quiet our minds during a few minutes of meditation. When I meditate, I often receive what I call "word bubbles" of wisdom. Sentences and paragraphs kind of appear in my head fully formed like word bubbles in a comic book. I always keep pen and paper next to me when I meditate, so I can write down whatever I'm given; unlike when I first started out, I now ask questions about what I'm receiving during meditation. This is something that I think many people don't realize they can do. We can ask questions, and that's one of the reasons I included exact transcripts of some of my automatic writing sessions in earlier chapters. I wanted to share some of my own back and forth conversations with Spirit, ones where I asked for clarification when I didn't understand something, so you could see what it's like.

When you sit down to meditate, ask your Higher Self (or your guide/angel) a question, or ask for guidance. Then sit quietly, clear your mind, breathe, and listen. You may get word bubbles like I do, or you might hear a voice, see pictures in your mind's eye, or even feel the answer—there's no right or wrong way to receive information during meditation. It's a very personal thing. What's important is that if you don't quite understand the message coming through mentally or verbally, clear your mind again, breathe, and wait for a response or clarification.

It sounds a little like I'm turning a meditation session into a channeling session. On some level, maybe that's true, but only because we don't really have a term to describe a meditative conversation with our Higher Selves. What's important here is that everyone reading this book is well beyond blindly receiving messages. Everyone reading this book is a high-powered, high-vibration entity who is fully able to turn a meditation session into a two-way conversation with Spirit. Again, as much as I love synchronicities, and I *do* love them, isn't it easier to ask what a message means instead of spending precious time trying to figure it out and hoping you have the right interpretation? When you hear a song five times, ask your Higher Self what it means. Seeing the number 333 everywhere? Ask your Higher Self, Guides, or Angels what it means. It's that simple, and I'm looking forward to your email saying, "Sherri, you were so right. I'm so glad I listened to you and started asking questions!"

**Chatting with Spirit Guides in Meditation**

We've been concentrating on talking with our Higher Selves, but we can and should also utilize meditation to help us meet and communicate with our Spirit Guides We accomplish this through *intention*. Here's how:

1. **Set the intention**. When we sit down to meditate, we announce to the universe, either verbally or mentally, that it is our INTENT to meet and receive a message from (fill in the blank) during our session.

2. **Tap into your inner power**. Direct your meditation session to meet or communicate with one of your Guides, your own guardian angel, or even Archangel Michael or Raphael.

3. **Allow yourself to receive**. Clear your mind, breathe, relax, and allow yourselves to be fully in the moment and at one with your INTENT for the meditation session.

To be completely forthcoming, when I want to talk with my Guides or even my mother or grandmother who are on the Other Side, I make my intention known and then communicate through the thought bubbles I talked about earlier or via automatic writing. I have never asked to speak with anyone that I don't know although from time to time, I have a new Guide or other entity pop in with information. When that happens, I ask them who they are and what their relationship is to me. If you don't know who you're communicating with, always ask who they are and what their relationship is to you—you'd ask a stranger who stops you on the street who s/he was, wouldn't you? You can also say a prayer of protection before you begin meditating. The one I use is on page 48.

# Chapter Six: Meditation

## What is Meditation?

Meditation is a state of awareness. The word "meditation" has its roots in Latin and means *to think and to heal.* I am not shy when it comes to suggesting to folks that they give meditation a try, and that's because I believe wholeheartedly that it is a tool that has both physical and spiritual benefits. Meditation assists us on many levels because it helps us learn to do the following:

1. **Focus our attention inward.** Some of the benefits of doing this are:
   a. improved ability to relax;
   b. inner calm that allows us to stop sweating the little things and put them into perspective; and
   c. increased ability to access the creative centers of our mind to resolve problems with greater insights.
2. **Heal our bodies and spirit through concentrated awareness.** This allows us to do the following:
   a. release pent-up or misplaced anger, ease stress, deal with grief, and face our fears—all of which lends itself to increased vibrational levels;
   b. learn the practice of "following our breath" (being aware of each inhalation and exhalation) during meditation, which teaches and allows us to practice proper breathing which leads to better health; and
   c. bring our minds and bodies into harmony on all levels by practicing proper breathing.
3. **Acquire ongoing opportunities to get to know ourselves better.** As a result of this, we are able to do the following:

a. tap into and better hear our inner guidance (Higher Self); and

b. attain an open and calm mindset that facilitates direct contact with our spirit Guides and Angels.

The hardest thing about meditation is *getting started.* Once you have a few sessions under your belt, you'll be a believer in daily meditation. It restores balance to your body and your mind, and it's better than taking a power nap! Start with five minutes and work your way up to twenty or thirty minutes a day.

Here are some basic instructions for meditation, followed by directions on how to meditate with intent, and two *meditation with intent* exercises. Use them as a starting place, and don't be afraid to rewrite them according to your needs and personality.

**Basic Meditation Instructions**

- Pick a time of day when you can sit in undisturbed silence for at least 15-20 minutes; try to meditate at the same time each day. Sit upright in a comfortable chair or lie on the floor or the couch; do whatever feels comfortable to you.
- Close your eyes and start to clear your mind. As thoughts come in, don't worry about it; just recognize them and send them away. You can think about those things later!
- If you want to initiate communication with a specific entity, state your intent: i.e., "During this session, I intend to speak with my Higher Self," or "During this session I intend to meet my Guide." Sit quietly for 15-20 minutes, breathe and listen.
- As you receive messages, ask for clarification or ask questions if you have them.
- When you're finished meditating, thank the entity you've been chatting with, and remember to blow out candles and incense if you used them.

**How to Meditate with Intent**

- To receive messages from Spirit during meditation, use *intent* to direct your session.

- As you sit down, state verbally or mentally your intent for the session: if you want to communicate with your Higher Self, Guides or an Angel, say so clearly. Then breathe, clear your mind, and listen.
- If you receive a message for which you need clarification, ask for it.
- Keep a journal of your messages for future reference.

**Meditation with Intent to Receive Guidance from Your Higher Self**

- Sit quietly on the floor or on a chair or lie down.
- Your hands can be folded together on your lap or resting palms up on your knees.
- Take a deep cleansing breath in and out.
- Take another deep breath in and out.
- You are part of your Higher Self; you are always connected to your Higher Self.
- Your Higher Self communicates with you every day, all day. All you need do is quiet your mind and listen.
- Allow this awareness and understanding to enter and permeate your body.
- Take another deep breath in and out, and clearly state, "During this meditation I intend to receive guidance from my Higher Self."
- Continue to breathe and follow your breath as you feel your vibrational level increasing.
- Continue to breathe as you open your mind and heart to the part of you that is always near and wants only the best for you.
- And now, relax fully as you continue to breathe. Listen with love as your Higher Self brings you the messages and guidance that will allow you to complete your goals for learning and growth.

**Meditation with Intent to Receive Messages from Your Guide/s**

- Sit quietly on the floor or on a chair.
- Make sure that your back is straight and your spine is erect.
- Your hands can be folded together on your lap or resting palms up on your knees.
- Take a deep cleansing breath in and out.
- Take another deep breath in and out.
- Mentally give your body permission to relax totally as you become aware of your body being supported by the earth.
- Allow this awareness to enter and permeate your body.
- Take another deep breath in and out and clearly state, “During this meditation I intend to receive messages from my Spirit Guide.”
- When Spirit connects with you, ask who is speaking with you, and what your relationship is.
- Follow your breath now as you continue to inhale deeply and exhale fully. Feel yourself open up to the sensation and power of your breath.
- Continue to breathe and listen as you open mind and heart to receive messages from your Spirit Guide.
- And now relax and commune with your Guide as you receive messages and ask questions.

Now that you have these meditation tools to add to your spiritual toolbox, the next chapter contains more tools to connect and communicate further with Spirit.

# Chapter Seven: Connecting to the Divine— Easier and Simpler Than You Think!

I asked my dear friend, Irene Lucas, author of *30 Miracles in 30 Days*, to write a guest chapter for this section about connecting to and communicating with Spirit. Irene has been a metaphysician for more than twenty-five years and writes and produces videos to empower people with developmental disabilities. I first met Irene at Ozark Mountain Publishing's 2010 Transformation Conference, where we were both speakers, and I was immediately attracted to her high-vibrational energy. I personally refer to Irene's book constantly, and I frequently use the meditations she included in *30 Miracles in 30 Days*. The chapter she's written for us below is like being in one of her powerful workshops.

Without further ado, here's Irene to give us some enlightening advice and a special five-step exercise to assist us in connecting with Spirit.

**Irene Lucas Shares How to Dance with the Light**

*Are you breathing? Do you have a pulse? So far, so good!*

*Dance with the Light in five simple steps.*

*Connect to the Divine and co-create the miracles your heart desires.*

You do not need other people to connect to Spirit for you—I used to think so. Let go of the erroneous belief that *other people* are more worthy—gifted, have an inside track, special knack, etc.—than you. Even if you hold that belief, press on anyway. You will be thrilled—as was I, and wow, what a huge relief!—when you discover that you (already) are a beloved, worthy, Divine co-creator and communicator with Spirit.

Whether you are aware of it or not, trust and faith are already alive within you, awaiting your conscious reconnection to your Divine Friends. You are always *already worthy*. You are always *already ready*.

As part of the One, each of us radiates the spark of Spirit within. Spirit, the Holy Masters, Angels and Archangels are all awaiting their turn to dance in the Light with you, revealing and cultivating your own *already present gifts!*

I speak from experience. I watched the train go by for a long time, thinking that I wasn't quite sufficiently worthy, ready, on time, etc., before I finally realized that all I had to do was *show up* at any moment, benefit from my experience of hesitation, and just jump on board. Divine arms are waiting to embrace you, and the ride is a lot of fun!

You are already "getting it right"! Accept and cultivate your own Divine spark. If you can breathe, you can connect to the Divine and co-create miracles. It really *is* that simple.

Simple tools = easy access.

Five simple steps from the Holy Masters (noted below) and your own authenticity are all you need.

Now is the moment!

In order to bring about shifts of energy, our Divine Friends await your invitation and with your permission, will guide their healing Light very deeply into all of your four bodies—mental, emotional, physical and spiritual, reawakening your very DNA.

Co-create your own miracles! You are the dance partner, the creator, the initiator. The Holy Masters and Archangels, so eager and delighted to lovingly serve, are even now awaiting your invitation and permission. Dance!

As you consider your miracles, the Holy Masters ask you to remember basic truths about yourself:

*Holy I Am. Worthy I Am. Divine Intervention, I Am.*

**Irene's 5 Steps to Co-create Unlimited Abundance, Healing and Health**

Let's have some fun! Your Divine Celestial Army and Personal Cheering Squad are eager and awaiting their turns! Each of the five steps is presented in-depth in the following meditation. Relax, enjoy, review and have fun.

1. **BEGIN HOLY BREATHING.** *So much simpler than it sounds, especially since you are breathing anyway!* Your breath is the Breath of Spirit.

    a. Breathe in. Breathe in Spirit. As deeply as you can, breathe in through your nose; then breathe out through your mouth.

    b. You are refreshed, revitalized, infused with the Divine energies.

    c. Breathe out any other energies, such as distracting thoughts, experiences, and/or emotions that do not serve to help you stay clear and focused.

2. **CLEAR AND CREATE YOUR OWN SACRED SPACE.** Whether you are in a calm space at home or surrounded by chaos and seemingly psychotic behavior anywhere from supermarket lines to traffic jams to office staff meetings and anyplace in between, clear and create your own sacred space!

    a. Accomplish this in a moment. Breathe, intend, pray, creating a physical sacred space as well as a sacred state of mind and grace.

    b. Call forth Divine White Light and breathe in the Light. Say or think "I bless this space as sacred." Breathe Spirit in. "I call forth St. Germaine and the Violet Flame of Transmutation." Breathe out. "I bless and send all energies into the Violet Flame."

3. **FOCUS AND FIND YOUR CLARITY OF INTENTION.**

    a. Use your best honesty and authenticity and have fun at the same time.

    b. What is your heart's desire, your clear intention?

    c. You do not sit at a restaurant table and simply ask for food and wait to see what arrives. You are specific in your intention and ask and inform carefully and specifically.

4. **INVITE AND ENVISION YOUR DIVINE FRIEND/S.** Rest. No need to compel, will, or achieve. Simply allow.

   a. Invite your Divine Friend/s.

   b. State the miracle/s you intend and/or your question/s clearly and specifically.

   c. Relax into the meditation—you are already Divinely supported! You don't have to be a tower of faith—just be willing to be willing!

5. **PRACTICE GRATITUDE AND PAY ATTENTION.** Make the leap to be alert and aware.

   a. With gratitude in your heart, listen for the answer/s to your question/s and watch for the miracles arriving in expected and unexpected ways.

   b. Offer your gratitude. Consider the matter *already complete* and wait for the miracle to unfold and manifest.

   c. Ignite your vision and intention with your own personal passion. Imagine how it feels to have already received the miracle!! The energy of gratitude is, in fact, its own Divine prayer.

It is not our job to control, take charge of or define the who, where or how of the outcome. We have only to allow, notice and be grateful for the miracles manifesting in our lives.

***Change is not enough.***

***Transformation is required.***

Mauve Ray: Clarity of Intention

Thank you, Irene, for this wonderful workshop! For more about the Mauve Ray and Clarity of Intention, please pick up a copy of Irene's book, *30 Miracles in 30 Days*. You'll be glad you did!

# Chapter Eight: Automatic Writing

Since making first contact with my Guide, Jeremy, through automatic writing in 1987, it's been a rare day that I haven't sat down to communicate with my Guides using this method. In fact, a great deal of the material that appears in my books was dictated to me by three different Guide Groups via automatic writing, and it remains my favorite way to communicate with Spirit.

It's my favorite way because all I have to do is sit with a pen and paper or at my computer and allow Spirit to write through me. I'm fully conscious while it's happening, so I can ask questions and request clarification about the information I'm receiving. It's very much a back and forth conversation. When I'm writing/receiving on the computer, it reminds me of instant messaging—it's that easy and that smooth. In my opinion, the best thing about automatic writing is that you have a written record of all the information and wisdom you're receiving—no straining the brain trying to remember everything that comes through. We can write with our Angels and our Guides, and many people also write with their Higher Selves. How do we know with whom we are writing? If you don't know, ask!

**Approaches to Connecting with Spirit via Automatic Writing**

I'm aware of three ways to use automatic writing to connect with Spirit:

1. It can be like dictation where you hear a voice and then write down what you hear. The voice can be inside or outside of your head, and it may or may not sound like your own voice.

2. Another way is when Spirit physically pushes or moves the pen in your hand or your hands on a computer keyboard.

3. Next is how it happens for me—a combination of the first two ways. I hear the words in my head in my own voice while at the same time my hands are being moved on the keyboard, or the pen is moved across the paper.

Something important to keep in mind is that what I experience is not the *right way* to experience automatic writing; it's simply *a way* to experience it. When I first began studying automatic writing and taking psychic development courses, I was absolutely obsessed with doing everything *right* and experiencing everything exactly the way my teachers taught it or the way I read it was done in books. I wasted a lot of time and effort worrying about getting it *right*, instead of simply enjoying the experience. We are all individuals, and Spirit is individual, too, this means that no two people will ever have the exact same experience. When you read my method later in this chapter, do so with the understanding that your experiences and mine are not supposed to be exactly alike. Know that you'll develop *your own* personal style and methodology.

Something I've found interesting about my experience is that when I'm communicating with my Higher Self, Guides, or other entities that have information for me, it may be my voice that I hear, but the words are strung together differently than I would say them. Also, the ideas are often given to me using words that I wouldn't think to use. For instance, Gilbert always begins his conversations with "Greetings!" and that's a term that would never come out of my mouth. And the original GG from *Windows of Opportunity* always ended their sessions with the words "Go in Peace"—not something that I would ever think to say.

The best advice I can ever give you about automatic writing is to have patience and perseverance. Don't give up. I first tried to do automatic writing back in the 80s after reading all the Ruth Montgomery books. I thought it was very cool how she sat down at her kitchen table and wrote with Spirit, and I wanted to do it, too. For months I sat at my kitchen table every morning, and nothing happened.

Then one night during a psychic development class, the teacher said, "Tonight we're going to try automatic writing." Interesting note: Sunna Rasch of the GG for this book (but who was still on *our* side of the veil at the time) was sitting next to me during this workshop as I started laughing out loud at the instructor's words.

Then, as the declaration, "That will never happen for me!" was exiting my mouth, I felt something grasp my hand, and I began drawing many, many beautiful scribbles and circles.

Everyone in the class was huddled around me watching my hand, and I was watching my hand, too. I was fascinated, and I remember thinking, "Oh, so this is what it's like!"

From across the room, I heard the teacher yell, "Sherri, control it!"

But I couldn't control it! I only knew what I knew from reading the Ruth Montgomery books, which was to sit down and hold a pencil.

I'm sure I yelled back, "How? We haven't had the class yet!" and then I just let it continue until it stopped a few minutes later.

Although I didn't know it at the time, it was Jeremy coming through that night. As I sat down daily to work with him, the circles turned into words, and eventually the words turned into books. Over time, many different entities came and wrote with me, giving me personal advice, wisdom and eventually enough channeled information to write three books. It's very important to me that you know that if *I* can use automatic writing as a means of communicating with Spirit, so can *you.*

I've been doing automatic writing since 1987. That's over a quarter of a century, and I continue to love the way it allows me to connect with Spirit anytime and anywhere. I've been known to pull my car over to the side of the road to ask a question, and I've even written on the palm of my hand when I didn't have paper available. There have been times when I've gotten what I can only describe as a knocking at my brain and knew that someone wanted to communicate with me. If I was at work, I'd head to the ladies room and into a bathroom stall with pen and paper and start writing. Yes, I have really done this!

As Doreen Virtue says, "Practice makes perfect" when it comes to automatic writing; the first step is, of course, *to make contact.* The next step is to become comfortable with the process, and before you know it, you'll be having meaningful conversations with Spirit. I've given the following instructions in both of my other books, but communicating with Spirit this way is so rewarding that I am compelled to give them again, so you can get started today!

**Getting Started**

Choose a time of day when you can sit undisturbed for at least 15 minutes; however, if nothing happens during the first five minutes, you can end the session. Nothing is going to happen at that time.

- Sit comfortably with a pad of paper on the table in front of you, and hold a pen or pencil loosely in your hand with the tip of your writing instrument touching the paper. You can use a computer keyboard instead of pad and paper.
- Say a prayer of protection. For example, "I am protected by the love of God. Only those entities of the highest intentions can pass through my door. If others should try, my door will immediately close, effectively blocking them out. This is my prayer of protection. Amen."
- Write on the top of the paper, "Will someone write with me?"
- Clear your mind and wait. If it helps you to burn incense or candles, go right ahead. Remember to blow them out when you're finished.

**Your First Connection**

- When you first connect, it may feel like someone is grasping your hand and/or your arm. It's different for everyone. Just relax—let it happen.
- You will most likely experience drawing/writing circles and/or figure 8s and back and forth movements with your pen or pencil. If you're on a computer, you may experience your fingers moving around on the keys before you actually start to type.
- Ask the entity for his/her name by writing the question on your paper or typing on the computer.
- Next ask the entity what his/her relationship is to you. Don't go any further until you know who you're writing with.

- Next, ask the entity for a message, i.e., "Do you have something to share with me?" Write this down on the paper and wait for a response.
- As you get information, you can ask questions about what you're receiving. It's important to write your questions down and wait for the responses. If you want to end a session, just write: "I have to go now."
- When your guide is finished, you'll feel your hand and arm relax. My Guides end our sessions with the words "Go in Peace" to signify the end of a session. You'll establish a similar type of routine with your guide/s. Always thank your Guide after each session.

**Continued Sessions**

Here are some things to keep in mind as you continue your automatic writing sessions:

- When you first begin, do your automatic writing at the same time each day. Have a set appointment time with your Guide/s.
- Keep in mind that your Guides have lives, too. If you can't make a session, let your Guide know you won't be working with him/her that day. Just say out loud, "I'm sorry. I can't make it today for our session."
- Meditate for a few minutes before you start your session—it will help you open up and keep focused.
- Say the prayer of protection before you start. It will keep you firmly in the Light.

There are so many ways to connect with Spirit that we haven't covered. Prayer and affirmations are two ways that I love as a means of focusing our attention, but they represent one-sided communication—and the goal of the GG, this book and me is to get you having back and forth conversations with Spirit. I love tarot cards, too, but if you don't read them yourself, it's difficult to converse with Spirit this way daily, and daily access to Spirit is something we all deserve and should all enjoy. It's what Spirit wants for us. It's what we were born to experience.

You know that I prefer straightforward back and forth conversations with Spirit. I like to communicate with my Guides like I'm at the kitchen table having tea or a glass of wine with an old friend. Once you develop your meditation and/or automatic writing skills and use them with intent, you will find yourself having very rewarding, insightful, and incredibly interesting conversations with your Higher Self, Guides, and Angels, too.

In many of her wonderful books, author and hypnotherapist Dolores Cannon indicates that as we evolve, the veil between those incarnated and those "not in body" continues to thin. The veil becomes thinner every day, and so communicating with Spirit becomes easier and something that we all can do on our own. All we have to do is focus our attention and intention on making it so.

# SECTION THREE

# WALK-INS

# Chapter Nine: More Souls "Walking in"

There's a lot of chatter about *walk-ins* these days, and you already know what the GG has to say about them: more and more souls are walking-into bodies that have become available because the original soul has transitioned.

GG: ***Walk-ins are here now in much greater numbers; the main reason that this is possible is because the vibrational level of this planet is such that entities can step down into an adult body with more ease than in previous decades. The fact that more are able to walk into a body is a tribute to the work that the Lightworker Brigade has done on planet Earth. Remember, Sherri, walk-ins are entities that have no need to go through the growing up period of life as human beings. By walking into an adult body, they can hit the ground running and accomplish much more in a shorter amount of time.***

***There are more higher-vibrational entities being born or walking in every day, and this is a direct reflection of the hard work of all who are presently incarnated. The Lightworker Brigade has earned many a spiritual medal for excellent service during this sojourn on planet Earth and many a spiritual purple heart as well. We applaud you all and give you a well-deserved standing ovation.***

*Walk-ins*, like Indigos, Crystals, and Rainbows, are able to be here en masse and do their work because the first waves of Lightworkers paved the way, and it's great to know that our hard work is paying off.

I first learned about *walk-ins* in the 1980s when I read Ruth Montgomery's books, *Strangers Among Us* and *Threshold to Tomorrow*. Shortly after I read these books, I saw a show on TV about a man who had a terrible accident—he was working under his car when the jack malfunctioned and the car fell and crushed him. He spent months in a coma, and when he awoke, it was like he was a completely different person. Upon awakening, his interests had completely changed, and he had an agenda that included making positive changes to help make the world a better place. His friends and family felt like he was a stranger. I immediately thought to myself, "I bet he's a *walk-in*!" And I wrote a letter to Ruth Montgomery asking for thoughts.

I hadn't thought about *walk-ins* for years. Then in early 2012 shortly before the GG started talking about them, I picked up a copy of Shirley Battie's wonderful book, *Spirit Speaks* (www.littleowl.org). As I was reading this book, my Guides communicated that there are more *walk-ins* here today than ever before, and then I received an email from someone who actually *is a walk-in*. The synchronicity of those three events led me to write three columns about *walk-ins* for Examiner.com. I then received many emails from people saying how much those columns helped them. As you will see in the pages that follow, some shared their own personal experiences and stories, and several agreed to allow me to print their experiences, wisdom and advice. We'll get to that shortly, but first, here's some basic information about *walk-ins* and *walk-in* situations.

**When Does a Walk-in Occur?**

A *walk-in* situation occurs when an evolved soul, who is not currently incarnated, is allowed to switch or exchange places with a soul that is currently incarnated. The two souls essentially change places, and they do so by mutual agreement—no one is forcing anyone out of his/her body so he/she can take it over, and there is no possession scenario happening.

**What Is the Purpose of a Walk-in Situation?**

A *walk-in* situation allows two souls to continue their journeys. Ultimately, it allows a highly evolved soul to enter as an adult and work to help others and our planet almost immediately. It's an agreement that is a win-win situation for both souls, albeit often confusing and difficult for the incoming soul and the outgoing soul's family and friends.

## Why Does a Walk-in Situation Occur?

A *walk-in* situation can occur when two souls, prior to incarnation, make an agreement that when the first soul has completed its development or spiritual To Do List, the second soul will takes its place. Another example would be that something may have happened to make the outgoing entity want to leave the body early, i.e., chronic illness or a tragic accident, so another soul will take over for the departing soul. *The walk-in soul is always one that is highly/sufficiently evolved enough to skip the birth process and enter at the adult stage of life.*

## Steps in a Basic Walk-in Situation

Here's a list of the basic steps that take place during a *walk-in* situation:

1. An agreement exists or takes place between two souls.
2. The two souls switch places.
3. The outgoing soul continues its journey and learning on the Other Side of the veil—just as we all do when our current incarnation is over—and can reincarnate again when ready to do so.
4. The *walk-in* must complete the karma of the outgoing soul; that is part of the agreement.
5. The *walk-in* has a specific mission, which can include teaching, assisting humankind in awakening, and/or helping individuals find their life purpose/path.

## Typical Characteristics of Walk-ins

As Shirley Battie writes in *Spirit Speaks*:

*How often have you heard of someone who survives a terminal illness and then has a new lease on life and goes on to raise funds or provide inspiration in one way or another? Often the individual seems changed in more ways than one to those who knew him or her?*

*A walk-in retains all of the memories and experiences of the soul with whom he/she has exchanged places, but sometimes there are glitches or behaviors that indicate an exchange has taken place.*

Here are some things to think about to help determine if you or someone you know is a *walk-in*:

1. You feel totally different; you never feel quite "yourself."
2. You feel uncomfortable or like an outsider when you're with your friends and family.
3. Your interests and hobbies have changed drastically.
4. You might have memory lapses regarding why you walked-into this new body, and you may have memory lapses when it comes to all the memories of the outgoing soul.
5. You find yourself wanting to help other people through volunteer work, raising funds, and just plan lending a hand.
6. You are very concerned about the state of the planet and want to help.

**Meet Sara, a Walk-in Here to Help Earth Evolve**

I first met Sara when she wrote to me about my first book. We started corresponding, became great friends, and eventually she opened up and shared with me that she's a *walk-in*. This is something that she was extremely hesitant to share, and I was honored that she chose to share her story with me. Sara is a Medium/Channeler, Reiki Master and Life Coach. She may be contacted at sara.universal.light@gmail.com, and what follows is an interview with her to help us understand what it's like to be a *walk-in* and why *walk-ins* are here.

SC: Sara, thank you for sharing your journey with my readers. Can you tell us exactly what a walk-in is?

Sa: *Walk-ins are enlightened highly-evolved beings, who, based on a pre-birth contract have been permitted to inhabit the body of another human being who wishes to depart. It is an agreement between two souls that when soul #1 (the host) has completed his/her development and is ready to move on; soul #2 (the walk-in) is then allowed to enter. There are many walk-in situations taking place now because there is urgency at this time to assist in the dimensional transition of the planet, and the work of a walk-in often involves several worlds at the same time. Walk-ins are awakening now and becoming aware of who they are so they can help Earth beings to remember their true Divine identity. Walk-ins are usually involved with a Council comprised of souls/entities from other worlds, and I am one of a Council of 12 here to assist humanity.*

SC: Do you know when you arrived in this body?

Sa: *I arrived on March 10, 1991. Two weeks prior to the transition between the two souls, a soul-braiding takes place—this is when the host soul braids with the incoming walk-in soul for a specific length of time. Soul-braiding allowed me as the walk-in to familiarize myself with the other soul. In my case, just as the transition was about to be complete, the outgoing soul began struggling with the finality of leaving the body as she was so strongly connected to her human side. The deceased grandmother of the outgoing soul got involved and assisted in the exchange, and with love soul #1 departed as pre-arranged. Not all walk-ins enter during a car accident or trauma; many walk-ins are now entering to assist mankind in the same gentle way that I entered.*

SC: What was it like when you woke up in your new body?

Sa: *When I woke up in the morning, I was very confused. I remember thinking, "What is this place?" and "Who is this man lying next to me?" Then a young, blonde-haired boy walked past the room, and said, "Hi, Mom." He was about fourteen at the time, and with this child, I could immediately relate, for he was an Indigo. He was a key for me. I realized the exchange had been completed, and it was now a time of adjustment.*

SC: Wow! Sara, what were you feeling during those first days and weeks?

Sa: *My relationship with the family changed. I recognized that they were now my family, and I had to look at and evaluate the situation. I had taken and retained the memories and all the responsibilities of the host/soul #1. I felt a great love for the family, for I work from my heart center. My relationship with my spouse changed because I now looked at life, as you would say, with different eyes, and I knew in the future that my relationship would be completed with this wonderful man. And in 1998, as difficult as it was, I ended the marriage and started on my own journey. My responsibility is to complete the host soul's karma, for I had entered with none.*

*I had watched mankind and what was happening to Mother Earth, and I just wanted to scream to the world "Wake up, people! Look at what's happening to your planet. Look at your relationships with one another."*

*It was very frustrating for me, and I communicated with my Council members on the Other Side that I could not believe what I saw happening on planet Earth even though I had previous knowledge.*

SC: Do you know what your mission/path is?

Sa: *Yes, my mission is to assist mankind in their awakening and their life purpose. Those whom I assist are generally not on their correct path and find their way to me for assistance with their journey. I also work as a medium. The bottom-line answer to your question is this: My mission is whatever is put upon my pathway for the service of humanity. I am a very humble soul in my work, for I never work from the ego because ego, to me, stands for easing God out. EASING GOD OUT. All mankind must learn to work from their heart center; that is the only way to ascend to 5D.*

SC: Sara, thank you so much for sharing this information. I know your words here will help many people who are also walk-ins or know someone who is a walk-in who is trying to figure out what's going on in his/her life. Is there anything else that you would like to share?

Sa: *Follow your path, my friends. Work only from your heart center, and everything else will unfold. I do remember one funny incident that I still laugh about to this day. The first time I walked around a mall, I noticed a sign outside a beauty salon that said, "Walk-ins Welcome." I felt at home on planet Earth!*

I'm so happy to share that Sara, who has become my dear friend—despite her insistence on Skyping at 6:00 A.M. when I have no makeup on and haven't combed my hair yet!—is pushing open the door to her spiritual closet to a much wider degree and is currently writing her own book and leading workshops.

**Meet Shirley Battie, Lightworker, Author, and Walk-in**

Synchronicity is an interesting thing. After I read Shirley's book, *Spirit Speaks*, I loved it so much that I wrote a review about it for Examiner.com and sent her a copy. Shirley started reading my columns, saw what I wrote about *walk-ins*, and wrote the following email to me, which I'm reprinting here with her permission and without editing:

*How odd that synchronicity comes yet again. You may, if you like, add my story about walk-ins. I had just closed my circle for Christmas. I was told by Spirit to hold a discussion on walk-ins that same week. I phoned my group, and they agreed to come even though we had no idea what it was about. That same week I had occasion to go to a crystal warehouse where the secretary walked up to me and said, 'You are a walk-in. Take this book by Ruth Montgomery, STRANGERS AMONG US.' That very same week I had an unplanned reading during which the medium said, 'I don't know who she is, but you will be introduced to someone called Ruth Montgomery.'*

*Well, three things in a row I could not ignore, so I wrote to Ruth Montgomery through her publisher saying I could not ignore such synchronicity and could we meet. Amazingly she wrote to me, and this was before Internet. She suggested I contact someone in Minneapolis who was running things there. I liked the voice immediately. She told me that by chance they were holding their first international conference in UK that year, and would I like to go and make my mind up about it. It was not too far from me, so I went. What followed led to many astounding things happening, too long to go into here. I have since attended and spoken at other Walk-in conferences and have made lots of friends.*

It's interesting that three occurrences led me to write columns about *walk-ins*, and three things led Shirley to write to Ruth Montgomery. I also wrote to Ruth Montgomery about *walk-ins* and received a reply from her as well. These synchronicities are examples of how we are all so very connected even though we don't realize it—kind of like that game, Seven Steps to Kevin Bacon.

I'm proud and honored to say that Shirley and I have become great friends. She's an international spiritual healer, teacher, clairvoyant, channeler, and the author of many important books (http://www.little-owl.org). When I told her I was working on this chapter, she graciously sent me the following information:

*Sherri, there are many who could be classed as walk-ins on the planet today. Many have no idea that they are such. If they feel they have changed dramatically after a traumatic time and now have a mission or an urge to do something to help others, then the chances are that they have had a change-over. It often ends a marriage or relationship because they are not what they were, or a relationship could change for the better when it hadn't seemed possible.*

*What is really important is not what you might be and where you have come from but what you do with your life and how you are as a person. Your soul's journey is the most important thing right now, no matter what body form you have taken on. Even if you shape-shifted and swapped bodies many times, it is still your own soul that is journeying and doing what it feels to be right.*

Thank you, Shirley!

**Aha! Moments of Walk-ins**

After I wrote my Examiner.com columns about *walk-ins*, I heard from many people who already knew they were *walk-ins*. I also heard from others who, after reading some of the characteristics of a *walk-in*, had that *Aha* moment and wrote to tell me about it. I took notice of several similarities in the stories that were shared with me and created a compilation of those that particularly stood out:

- Several wrote about reading the Ruth Montgomery books and recognizing themselves in her words. There is no doubt that Ruth Montgomery influenced many of us and helped us embark on our spiritual paths.
- Similarly many folks expressed gratitude for Dolores Cannon (www.Ozarkmt.com), her hypnotherapy work and eye-opening books where they learned so much about *walk-ins*, our planet, and the universe in general.
- Nearly every single *walk-in* that wrote to me mentioned seeing a sign in a shop that read "Walk-Ins Welcome" and said they felt it was a special message that brought tears to their eyes.
- Every single person that wrote to me also expressed an intense desire to heal planet Earth.
- 100% of those that reached out to me said that at first, they felt like strangers in their new bodies and among their family and friends, too. They said they immediately began the business of tying up loose ends for the previous occupant, which often included making life-changing decisions that drastically altered the life course of the previous occupant of the body.

I love the fact that *walk-ins* like seeing those little signs in shop windows and that authors Ruth Montgomery and Dolores Cannon play such a big part in their lives. It's these types of synchronistic happenings that remind us that there is a definite plan in action for our lives, and that we are all connected.

Why are Sara, Shirley, and many, many others *coming out* and sharing their stories with us now? Because they want to help our *walk-in* population realize they're not alone and to help all of us understand what's going on in our world as the human race continues to evolve.

# SECTION FOUR

# MAKING THE MOST OF THIS INCARNATION

# Chapter Ten: Living in the Here and Now

The GG mentioned the importance of living in the *here and now* several times earlier in this book. Centering our attention and staying focused is important to us because making the most of the *here and now* is clearly part of a Lightworker's overall mission. The question that's begging to be asked here is "What can we as Lightworkers do to facilitate our evolution?" Three actions come to mind:

- Be present.
- Live in the moment.
- Watch what we think and say.

We've all heard these phrases over and over again. Maybe we've heard them so much that we start to wonder if they are truly powerful expressions or northing but clichéd New Age slogans. A cliché is a phrase that was originally used because it was so striking in its meaning. It is also a phrase that ends up being well-used because everyone who hears it immediately understands its meaning. Knowing this, I would not mind in the least if these three phrases, which contain important wisdom, become part of our everyday lexicon.

So, cliché or not, being present, living in the moment, and watching what we think and say are the heart and soul of our ability to live in the *here and now*. According to the GG, to live in the *here and now* is a crucial part of our spiritual growth, both individually and collectively. As we incorporate the above actions into our daily lives, we are, in fact, *practicing awareness*. We can't be present, be in the moment and watch what we're thinking and saying without being aware of exactly what we're doing, and if we're aware of what we're doing at any given moment, we will accelerate our progress. If we adopt these possibly "clichéd" sayings as part of our personal spiritual philosophy and add them to our daily routines, I believe the following will occur:

1. We will be living much more in the *here and now*;
2. We will quickly find ourselves spotting our "windows of opportunity" and crossing things off our spiritual To Do List much more swiftly; and
3. We will naturally boost the positive energy we create, *and* diminish the negative energy we churn out into the world.

At the 2011 Ozark Mountain Publishing Transformations Conference, I spoke at length about the fact that I had been on a "living in the *here and now* crusade" of sorts for several months—not just because of the great benefits that awareness brings to us but also because I felt then and still feel like there's a kind of soul-sickness among Lightworkers these days. I call this nasty little virus the "Rapture Bug," and those of us who have it, need to treat it immediately. Let me explain. I've received many emails and letters and read lots of posts online from folks who say that they are just "waiting for the rapture" or "waiting for their vibration level to speed up" so they can leave here and be part of 5D Earth.

When I hear someone say, "Oh, I just want to transition," or, horror of horrors, "I don't want to do anything; I'm just waiting to transition," I have to share with you that I get tears in my eyes, and my heart just breaks. I want to track these folks down and grab them and shake them *until they remember how important they are to the here and now*—not only to themselves but to <u>all</u> of us—because we're all connected. We need each other to move forward.

To be perfectly honest, I've had these same feelings myself. I long to be part of a world where human beings don't eat animals, animals don't eat other animals, and no one and nothing has to eat another living thing. I want to live someplace where the air is our food. That's my dream world. We all have a picture in our heads of the dream world that we want to be part of, and we're all working so hard to raise our vibrations and evolve. Yet I'm strongly suggesting to all the vital and essential Lightworkers reading this book to please consider living in the *here and now* even though I know that there isn't one of us that doesn't yearn to be someplace where there is no torture, no war, no hunger, no death, and no grief. But my dear friends, my fellow Lightworkers, that is *not* what we signed up for. And we cannot afford to give in to such feelings.

I've read many descriptions of what it will be like to live in 5D. I've even gotten some info about it from my Guides, which you can find in *Raising Our Vibrations for the New Age*. I love to read about it, and who among us doesn't want to be 5D? Truly though, you are already 5D and beyond and *stepped down* to 3D to do the work that's so necessary for humankind to evolve here. We remember on a soul level what 5D is like, and being Lightworkers, we want to create and live in a better world, which is fine. The thing that scares me is that some of us are deciding to allow things like waiting for a better world or for the shift to be complete or to transition to 5D to take the place of living our lives in the *here and now*. By now, we know that we are not going to disappear from the face of this Earth and wake up tomorrow on another *better Earth*. Some of us *have* transitioned, and there's no doubt that others will transition in the future, thus making their bodies available for other souls to *walk-in*, but it's time to put the fairy tale to rest. The personality/ego that we are right now in this incarnation is not going to instantaneously transition to 5D Earth.

And so I say to you that if we allow ourselves to yield to the "Rapture Bug," if we stop living our lives to the fullest, if we allow our thoughts to focus on "getting out of Dodge," if we make a conscious decision to do nothing but wait to transition to a higher vibration, well . . . in my humble opinion, we are committing "spiritual suicide."

How so? We have contracts to be here to do certain things. By completing our contracts, we are taking care of our own agenda while at the same time furthering the evolution of our current species. This is an important historic mission that we're on, but somewhere, somehow, many of us started to believe that the evolution of the human race to 5D status is the "be-all, end-all" of our mission. This is simply not true. It is also part of our mission to raise the vibrational level of 3D Earth to make this plane of existence less dense and to bring as much light here as we possibly can.

We all came into these bodies with a plan of action. We are all here to have experiences for learning and growth. When it comes to this learning, not only are we integral to our own learning experiences, but—important to remember—we also participate in and facilitate learning for our family, friends, and even strangers that we bump into on the street or meet in the grocery store.

As if these reasons aren't important enough to concentrate on the *here and now*, Lightworkers have three additional jobs so that human beings will continue to evolve:

- drawing 5th dimensional light to this planet;
- increasing positive energy; and
- decreasing negative energy.

My Guides have often talked about how difficult it is for Lightworkers given that we have so much more on our plates because (1) we *are* aware of our on-going evolution and (2) because we *are* 5D and beyond when we're not on planet Earth. These things make it easy for us to be bitten by the "Rapture Bug" and wile away our days and nights dreaming of better frequencies to come. When we start to feel this way—and if we're honest with ourselves, we all have days when we feel this way—let's quickly squash the "bug" by remembering the following:

1. **We are Lightworkers**.

    - We signed up to be here on 3D Earth to do the following: learn and grow here, help each other learn and grow here, and help humankind evolve here on 3D Earth.
    - Giving up on 3D Earth because we long to be part of 5D Earth or want to *go home* is not an option.
    - Our job is to make 3D Earth a better place, whether we have future incarnations here or not.

- This planet is counting on us!

2. **We are Warriors.**

- We are warriors on the front line of an amazing evolution.
- Many who wanted to be here physically to be part of this historic time in history couldn't get a body.
- Thus we are here on the *front line* of this incredibly amazing transformation and evolution.
- We owe it to ourselves and those who couldn't be here with us to take advantage of the opportunities for learning and growth that are in front of us NOW.

## Six Things We Can Do to Help Us Live in the Here and Now

I'm convinced that living in the *here and now* is the most important thing we as Lightworkers can do now to help ourselves, each other, our planet and humankind, too. And because I love lists, here are six actions that we can incorporate into our lives to help us remain firmly in the present:

### 1) Choose to spend your time with positive people.

One of the best ways to stay focused on the *here and now* is to hang out with positive people—people who are determined to make the most of each day, folks who wouldn't entertain the thought of stepping foot on "Poor Me Avenue," and those who are not stuck in the past continually reliving unpleasant events. Hang with people who will slap the "Rapture Bug" right off your shoulder should it land on you so it won't become a permanent chip compromising your spiritual growth and your evolutionary mission.

My day job is Director of Specialty Sales for a large vacation resort in Orlando, Florida. The number one reason that our sales reps fall into slumps is because they "neg each other out"—one rep is having a bad day, week or month, and he starts infecting the rest of the sales floor with his negativity. That one negative rep can pull a dozen or more reps down into the tar pit with him in less than an hour, which can adversely affect sales for the day. Negative vibrations are insidious, and in my experience, they multiply faster than positive vibrations. So hang out with positive people, and get up and walk away when Debbie Downer tries to infect you.

**2) Practice mindfulness.**

Another way to stay present and in the moment is to really focus on what you're doing. I mentioned earlier that when I was in college, I took a class called Meditation East and West. In that class we studied the great Vietnamese Buddhist monk, teacher and peace activist, Thích Nhất Hạnh, who was a pioneer in the development of western Buddhism and western meditation. He brought us the practice of *mindfulness.* In Buddhist meditation practices, mindfulness, which is also translated as *awareness*, is considered to be of great importance on the path to enlightenment. Mindfulness is difficult to define; it's hard to put into words, but basically, establishing mindfulness in one's day-to-day life means maintaining a calm awareness of one's body, feelings, thoughts and perceptions. In other words, being present in the moment and paying attention to your senses: *being profoundly alert* to your senses of touch, sight, smell, sound, and taste, and how you feel at any given moment.

The textbook we used in class said to practice mindfulness in all things, including when you're doing chores like washing the dishes, and if you couldn't do that, then you shouldn't wash the dishes. I laughed when I read that and *did not buy into mindfulness* right away. It wasn't until many years later that the light bulb went off in my head, and I went back and reread The Miracle of Mindfulness that the wisdom of mindfulness clicked in for me.

Are you ready for the two-part **secret** to bringing *mindfulness* to everyday chores like washing dishes? Here it is.

- View the chore as a positive event. Make it an exercise in self-understanding and stress relief.
- As you do the chore, focus on what you're doing—and nothing else.

For example, feel the warm slippery soapy water on your hands as you wash the dishes. Enjoy the warmth, texture and smell of the laundry as you fold it, and hear the sound of the birds when you step out the door in the spring. Feel the breeze or heat or cold on your face and hear the sound of your shoes as they hit the pavement as you walk through the parking lot to your car. In other words, use your senses to be in the moment.

Meditation is also a great way to practice mindfulness, as is deep breathing, which, of course, you can do while you're meditating. Listening to music can be an exercise in mindfulness if you truly focus on the sound and vibration of each note, the feelings that the music brings up within you, and other sensations that are happening as you listen.

I'm sure you can come up with lots of ways to practice mindfulness in your daily routine. I have, and I'm now so good at it that I jump out of my skin when my husband says something to me while I'm sweeping the floor or pulling weeds in the garden.

**3) Smile.**

Another way to be in the moment is to smile. We all know that smiling creates endorphins in our bodies and makes us feel happy. So when we smile at someone, we are not only focusing our attention and awareness on that individual, we're also doing something to elevate our own mood, as well. Here are some smiling exercises that we can all practice every day.

☺ Smile with your eyes as well as your mouth, and you'll really feel the joy.

☺ Smile when you wake up in the morning and you'll set a tone for appreciation and awareness that will last all day long.

☺ Smile and be mindful of how it makes you feel.

☺ Smile and be mindful of the reaction of the person or persons you just smiled at.

Smiling is an exercise that will help you focus, become more aware of your feelings, and increase your vibrations all at the same time.

**4) Practice random acts of kindness.**

Another thing we can do to be present in the moment is to practice random acts of kindness. In *Raising Our Vibrations for the New Age*, Gilbert channeled the following advice:

Gil: ***Practice Random Acts of Kindness. Doing so will create an immense outpouring of positive energy into the atmosphere. During random acts of kindness, people aren't thinking about the past or the future. They are having an exchange that is firmly in the present and has their attention focused on the present. This is great because so many have a hard time living in the moment, living in the present. With an act of kindness, you are a lighthouse emanating positive energy—you create a positive field around yourself and the person you are in contact with. This positive energy continues to emanate around you and positively affects others that you come into contact with, creating a domino effect. So random acts of kindness—seeing things that need to be done to help people, to help animals, to help the planet, and then acting on what you perceive, well, that's a dynamic way to increase vibrational levels.***

Really, what can I add to Gilbert's words except that random acts of kindness pack a double vibrational punch—they help us stay in the moment while allowing us to raise our vibrations.

**5) Take care of Mother Earth**.

We are not living on 5D Earth. We are living on 3D Earth, and 3D Earth is NOT a garbage can. Cleaning up after ourselves and others, if necessary, is what we need to do to keep our planet clean. As we pick up litter and as we recycle, we can focus on the following:

- what we're doing,
- the effect it's having, and

- how it makes us feel *to be part of the solution* instead of part of the problem.

I'm sure that no one told you that part of your job description as a Lightworker is to pick up garbage, but there you have it! If you see it, pick it up. It will keep you in the *here and now*, raise your vibrations, and help the planet at the same time.

**6) Pay attention to our thoughts and words**.

To say the right thing at the right time, we must be focused. When we focus on our thoughts and words, we automatically decrease the negative energy that would have been created by saying the wrong thing or saying the right thing in a snarky way. If we are sincere, we'll increase positive energy by saying nice things. This action item would not be complete without a few more words of wisdom from Gilbert.

Gil: ***It is important to reiterate that thoughts are things and will manifest much more quickly now than ever before. Imagine vibrating at 5D energy and thinking violent thoughts. In 5D, thoughts and words become reality almost instantaneously. Train yourselves NOW to govern your words and thoughts so that you actively contribute to making your 3D home a better place to live..***

As I was working on this section, I noticed an interesting trend. The things that help us raise our vibrations also help us stay in the moment. And with the former list, the GG intends for us to realize the tremendous amount of power we have to affect change, starting with living in the moment—a.k.a., the *here and now*. As Gilbert says:

Gil: ***Sherri, it takes courage and determination to make changes in one's life. Taking action is always more difficult than standing still and waiting for things to happen.***

Every single one of us possesses the courage and determination needed to be present, live in moment, and take charge of our thoughts and words. After all, we are Lightworkers, and together we will make 3D Earth a better place to live as we simultaneously work on our spiritual To Do List and continue to raise our vibrations.

**Our Responsibility to Our 3D Selves & 3D Earth**

**Newsflash #1:** 5D Earth already exists!

**Newsflash #2:** 3D Earth continues to exist!

**Newsflash #3:** If you're reading this book, you are on 3D Earth, and 3D Earth is our focus!

Just because 5D Earth already exists doesn't mean that 3D Earth ceases to evolve. That is simply not true, and aren't we proof of this? 3D Earth is most certainly continuing to evolve, and as Lightworkers, it's extremely important that we continue to do our jobs. We have a responsibility to help 3D Earth continue to evolve and to make the most of our 3D lifetime here on 3D Earth.

If you're feeling disappointment because you haven't transitioned to 5D, I have three words for you—the same three words the GG said to me. "Get over it." They said this to me in the nicest possible way, and I intend them for you in the nicest possible way. I know they sound harsh, especially coming from me, but for this discussion, I have to be tough. That said, there is no doubt in my mind that our souls will incarnate on 5D Earth the next time around *if* that's what *we* decide is the best thing for our personal growth.

Remaining here doesn't mean that you aren't the greatest Lightworker in the universe; it simply means that your work here isn't finished, or you committed yourself to complete your current incarnation here. Why would you leave before you finished your work? You would never do a thing like that! Here's more from the GG about those of us who remain on 3D Earth:

GG: ***Sherri, there are many on 3D Earth who have reached the vibrational level necessary to transition, and while their egos are disappointed that they are still here, their souls understand why they chose to stay put. This is a very important world and to abandon it makes no sense. This world continues to evolve, lessons continue to be learned, and experiences for growth continue to take place. Please remember that the whole of the Lightworker brigade—including the Indigos, Crystals, and Rainbows—can certainly transition, but what is the point when there is work to be done here? We know that you are feeling a bit betrayed because we have so often spoken of what 5D planet Earth is like, and you are very much a part of 5D Earth. We have told you frequently that Lightworkers spend much time there during their sleep state.***

***Should you and by "you," we mean all Lightworkers, truly wish to transition, you can do it. Your Higher Self would plead with you not to do so, however, and so it becomes a tug of war between your ego and your Higher Self. What we would say to the Lightworkers who are suffering from what you so eloquently refer to as the 'Rapture Bug' is this: Your Higher Selves have expressions on 5D Earth and also continue to have 3D expressions because there is still work to do here. Think of the chaos that would ensue here. Think of the windows of opportunity that would suddenly be gone and the carefully designed life plans that couldn't be carried out if ego would overtake the Higher Self and mass transitions would take place. 5D Earth and the evolved human beings who live there are the results of your hard work. You have much to be proud of, but if your work here isn't finished, then the likelihood of your simply transitioning to 5D is, well, unlikely. Paying attention to the here and now is the highest and best use of your time.***

Even the GG is a bit tougher in this book, aren't they? Let's talk about the "Rapture Bug" a bit more since the GG have brought it up again. We all long for 5D Earth, don't we? I know I do. We've worked hard to raise the vibrations of the human race to help the human race evolve, and we've read so much about the way human beings will/are living there. Of course we want to be part of it, and we addressed that desire earlier when we talked about that nasty little virus that I call the "Rapture Bug." And since the GG brought up that bug again, one more warning will not hurt. If you have this bug or know someone who is coming down with it or already has it, treat it immediately. If you don't have it, the time is now to strengthen your spiritual immune system so you don't contract this malicious bug. My dear friends, if we don't take action to keep it from attaching itself to us or if we don't detach it post-haste, it will prevent us from fully taking advantage of the bodies and lives we currently enjoy.

Let's end this section with a message from the GG:

GG: ***It is disappointing, we know, to work so hard and find that there is still so much more work to be done. You were chosen for this work and to be part of this brigade because of your strength and your experience. It is no easy task to be a Lightworker. When you feel down, we ask that you meditate and tune in to your Higher Self. Tell your Higher Self exactly how you feel and then be still and listen to your Higher Self communicate to you the great love that it has for you and how important you are to this mission. Your Higher Self is a great source of positive energy and encouragement that can be tapped into anytime you need it.***

## ***Make-Sense*** **Ways to Take Care of Our Planet (This One—The One We're On—in <u>This</u> Dimension!)**

As I write these words, Earth Day is just two days away. Here we are on planet Earth, a planet we very much wanted to be on at this time in history, and an appropriate question to ask ourselves is this: are we doing everything we can to help our planet? Why ask this question? Because looking after the health and well-being our planet is part of our job as Lightworkers.

Let's talk Earth Day. April 22, 1970, was the first Earth Day ever, and I was twelve years old and in seventh grade. Even at that young age, I remember thinking how exciting it was to have a day to celebrate the Earth. There were lots and lots of people making posters and talking about it at my junior high school, and we formed clean-up crews to get out there and make a difference for our planet.

That was forty-three years ago, and the creation of Earth Day marked the beginning of the environmental movement. It was founded by then Wisconsin Senator Gaylord Nelson in response to the 1969 oil spill in Santa Barbara and the student anti-war movement that was happening at the time. Nelson's idea was to combine the energy and focus of the students with the emerging public consciousness about pollution in order to inspire all of the existing conservation groups to work together. It worked, and the first Earth Day led to the creation of the United States Environmental Protection Agency, as well as the passage of the Clean Air, Clean Water, and Endangered Species Acts.

Speaking from a metaphysical point of view, it makes perfect sense that Earth Day was created during a time when a wave of Lightworkers commonly known as *Hippies* was working hard to change systems and paradigms that were standing in the way of the evolution of the human race. Earth Day was a radical idea in 1970. The idea of raising our vibrational levels and becoming 5th dimensional human beings is a radical idea today. All change starts somewhere, and here on Earth, it starts with a collective commitment to make the human race and planet Earth better, stronger, and something *more* than ever before.

The GG tell me that if we are still here, we are going to finish our incarnation here—no matter how much we might want to blink our eyes or wiggle our noses and transition to 5D Earth. We're here because we have work to do, and there are things we can do to help our planet in addition to pumping out positive energy on a daily basis, watching our thoughts, words, and actions, and focusing on the *here and now.* In fact, why *not* create a mindset and intention of *doing* at least one nice thing for our planet every day?

On Earth Day 2012, some of the lovely, caring folks who are part of my Facebook author page posted suggestions and shared the things that they're doing to help the planet. I'm so happy to share this list of ideas to help motivate us as we create our new mindset and set our intentions to help *our* planet every day:

- **Suzanne Miller of Philadelphia, PA**: *My awareness of Mother Earth has changed many of my behaviors. Let's try walking more or carpooling. I do not support any food suppliers that use pesticides, and I pick up trash in the street.*

- **Bex Gibbons of New Zealand**: *My family and I love doing beach cleanups at least every other weekend. We always find treasures, and the kids and I discuss how far what we've picked up has traveled and what damage it could have done to different creatures of the sea.*

- **Vickie Stover-Carlstrom of Satsuma, FL**: *For Earth Day I held a little celebration at Bloomers Garden Center where people gathered and spoke of water conservation, the importance of native plants and their "job" on our planet, and bees and the role they play in pollination. We also had the lovely Adele speak with interested folks about herbs and their healing powers. Mostly though, we celebrated our children, the next generation, and how, if taught how, they could make such a difference. There was plenty to speak about, and hopefully we got at least one person interested in helping save our planet. My suggestions are to re-cycle, re-use and re-purpose. Picking up trash is something that I also do. I know I feel guilt every time I drink bottled water. Everyone always wants to blame high fuel costs on the politicians when if we would just stop and think about when we were younger, we did not use so many products with plastics. I still believe that here in Florida we need to get back into recycling glass and plastics for cash. Think of the jobs that would be created, not to mention the litter removed from our roadsides.*

- **Carolyn Duff Laughlin of Fishers, IN**: *I TRY to do what I can for our Earth, and I always try to pick up litter wherever I am. Like, if I'm walking into the store and I see a piece of trash in the parking lot, I pick it up and put it in the trashcan by the door. If I see trash and can't get to it, like when I'm driving, I always say in my head, "Bless that piece of trash and bless whoever picks it up." May be silly, but it makes me feel better about not being able to get it myself.*

- **Heidi Winkler of Hawi, HI**: *I changed all the old-style lightbulbs in my house to the energy-saving light bulb, and I've stopped using paper napkins. I carry a plastic bag with me wherever I go and pick up garbage on the ground.*

- **Sara Achor of Columbus, Ohio**: *I recycle and walk to places when possible, and try to combine trips when I drive to save gas/reduce emissions. Recently, though, I signed up with a local produce co-op that I feel really good about: for $35.00 a week, I get a bin of produce delivered to my door which is, for the most part, organic and/or sustainably grown. The quality and variety has been just great so far, and no more expensive than if I was going to the grocery store myself. I feel like I'm helping out farmers who are growing things the right way, and I'm eating better because I have all this great stuff in my refrigerator!*

- **Cherie Kiley of Brockton, MA**: *Instead of using landscape fabric, I use paper bags in my gardens. I wet the ground, lay down a couple of layers of wet bags, and top off with mulch. The bags stay wet and prevent weeds from coming up.*

- **Lisa Crowder of DuPont, WA**: *I believe that buying locally is a great way to help our planet, and farmers markets are an amazing way to buy locally. My family and I enjoy the local farmers markets in the South Puget Sound area, where the kids and I can buy some veggies and bread and sit down on the shoreline to have a picnic. Buying locally means that local farmers/artisans are supported, people who don't use pesticides or use mass production methods that can strip the land and cause environmental waste. This method also cuts out the environmental effects of shipping the goods across the country to consumers. Buying locally also gives more people the space to be creative and open their own businesses. This creativity leads to more positive change in all areas.*

- **Shannon Carpenter of Springdale, AR**: *This isn't my idea, but I thought it was interesting. I watched a movie on Netflix this week called "Chemerical." It's a documentary about a family that is challenged to go chemical-free. They had to make their own soaps, laundry detergent, toothpaste, cosmetics, etc. At the end of the movie there was a suggestion for viewers to have a screening* *party of the movie for their friends and family, and afterward everyone would try making their own products. Another thought I had is to sponsor the spaying/neutering for a cat or dog at your local shelter (of course, after your own are "fixed").*

- **Viki Viertel of Lakeland, MN**: *I bring my own bags to the grocery store.*

- **Jennise Davis of St. Albans, NY**: *A simple way I help the Great Mother is I walk around and thank her. I send her love, light, and gratitude for giving us a stage to play out all of our dreams. I literally hug trees, apologize to plants I have mistakenly uprooted, and take caution not to feed the earth with recycled negativity that I may have picked up from anyone else. I re-use as much as possible. I also send negativity to her crystal core for transformation. And I stopped consuming animals.*

- **Teresa Moris of Glenhaven, WI**: *My advice is ...Just BE! Stop working so hard. Stop doing so much. Stop wanting so much. Eliminate negative people and situations from your life, ASAP. So how does this help the planet? When you Just BE, you become less stressed, which leads to being happier with yourself, which leads to being happier with others. Simply BE responsible for you own happiness, and then everything will be in Divine Flow! And that is how this simple statement of Just BE can help our planet.*

- **Sue & John Brennan of Orlando, FL**: *We use a rain barrel to catch rainwater to water our potted plants, compost kitchen and yard waste to put back into the vegetable garden, catch the cold shower water while waiting for the warm water to come use it to either flush the toilet or water plants, keep the AC at 81 when home—82 or 83 when away, and sprinkle used coffee grounds around the yard to add nutrients and have less to throw in the garbage.*

- **Stacy Herr of Lancaster, PA**: *One thing that I think will help the Earth tremendously is teaching our children. Their pure light, laughter and unconditional love heals like nothing else! My boys hug trees, dig in the dirt and plant seeds. I try to show them the beauty in nature, in all creatures, to appreciate life in general. I believe that this helps heals the Earth.*

- **Chere Menville of Clearfield KY**: *Here are some ideas for recycling that I use:*

  - *Turn milk jug rings and metal bottle caps into wind chimes. Milk jug rings also make great tiny dream catchers—which make nice gifts, and they can also be used to make beautiful earrings and necklaces.*

  - *Milk jug caps can be used for putting under furniture legs to keep from scratching up your floor when moving them or for balancing that chair leg that wobbles.*

  - *Milk Jugs make excellent penny banks, and you can write a dream on the side of the jug (like a wishing jug) and place your coins in a small slot close to the top.*

  - *Boxes: Empty boxes, such as trash bags, cereal (like oatmeal packet boxes) and the like can be used as coupon collectors, box top and label savers or a temporary bill and mail sorters.*

  - *Coffee cans with lids can be used as a personal compost maker, just add veggie scrapes, egg shells, coffee grounds. They can be later added to soil and covered by dry fall leaves. Shovel-stir in the spring, and you have your own compost to fuel your garden.*

  - *Used water bottles can be filled with water and turned upside down with the opening quickly placed in the soil of big potted plants when you are going to be away or are always forgetting to water your plants. The roots will slowly pull the water from the bottle as needed.*

  - *Newspapers and pizza boxes—I use these to line around my plants and weight them down with stones and recycled boards to line my garden and prevent weeds from taking over.*

  - *Soup and vegetable cans—I decorate these and use them for pencil/pen holders.*

So many great ideas that are so easy to incorporate into our daily lives! Many thanks to all who contributed! To those of you reading this book, I would love to have your ideas to share on my Facebook page. Please take time to email me at www.SherriCortland.com.

Now feel free to laugh at me as I tell you this story. About eight years ago, I remember thinking to myself, "Wouldn't it be great if I could use this paper plate again? They should make a plate that can be reused." And then I realized how crazy that sounded and stopped using paper plates and paper cups altogether. Yes, it takes a couple of minutes to wash the dishes, but it's worth it to cut down on the amount of trash going into the landfills. Like Suzanne, Bex, Vickie, and Heidi, I also pick up garbage from the ground—and I'm still amazed at the "what the heck are you doing" looks I get while I'm doing it. I also stopped washing most of my clothes in hot water; I'll still use hot water for whites, but that's about it. The minute I read Cherie's delicious nugget about laying down wet bags instead of landscape fabric, I couldn't wait to put it to use.

In preparation for this chapter, I've done some research and compiled a list of some additional Earth-saving actions that will give Mother Earth the helping hand she deserves. None of these take a lot of time to do or cost a lot of money; in fact, some of them will save us money. Take a look and see what you think:

1. **Re-use gift bags and wrapping paper.** I've been doing this for many years now, and sometimes, I'll even use leftover holiday paper for birthdays. No one has complained about it yet!

2. **Shop at garage and yard sales and have a garage or yard sale.** I've found "cat trees" that go for $300 in catalogs for $10, planters that would cost $20-30 in the store for a dollar or two apiece at garage sales and lots of other great bargains. Garage sales save space in our landfills. If you have a lot of stuff, and you don't want to have a garage sale, invite your friends over to take what they want or donate it to a charitable organization.

3. **Buy re-useable bags for your groceries.** When my husband, Ted, and I first started to do this several years ago, we got a lot of strange looks from the cashiers at the grocery store. Now nearly every store we shop at sells reusable cloth bags.

4. **If you buy bottled water, switch to a brand that uses recycled plastic in its bottles.** Better yet, get a permanent water bottle and keep it filled with filtered water or even tap water. I started doing this several years ago with plain old tap water.

5. **Run as many errands as possible in one trip.** I do everything that has to be done on one side of the road first, and then hit everything on the other side on the way back. Bundle errands by geographic location, and you'll save time and gas.

6. **Recycle your old cell phones.** If they go to the dump, they stay there for years as their batteries exude toxic substances into the landfill. Lots of great organizations are looking for cell phones; try donating them to groups that help battered women.

7. **Stop using plastic containers.** Switch to re-useable containers. My friend, Sue Brennan, brings re-usable containers with her when we go out to eat—so much better than taking leftovers home in a Styrofoam container.

8. **Don't throw away paper if you can use the back of it as scrap paper.** I've been known to cut 8 ½ x 11 scrap paper in half or quarters, and staple 20-30 pieces together to make mini-scrap pads.

9. **Use a mug at work instead of Styrofoam.** I hate washing my mug. I really do, but when I think about the benefit to the planet of cutting back on Styrofoam, I'm happy to rinse it out.

10. **Use cotton swabs with a paperboard spindle.** According to a website called Fifty Ways to Help the Planet (http://www.50waystohelp.com), "Some brands of cotton swabs have a paperboard spindle while others are made of plastic. If 10% of U.S. households switched to a paperboard spindle, the petroleum energy saved per year would be equivalent to over 150,000 gallons of gasoline." I've already made the switch.

11. **Place a brick or similarly voluminous object in the tank of your toilet.** By displacing some of the water, there's less of it to

flush each time. See this website for more ideas: http://www.treehugger.com.

12. **Save money and reduce electricity usage.** "Vampire Electricity Leaching" is responsible for 10% of your electric bill. Keep that 10% for yourself by unplugging unused appliances and electronics when not in use; i.e., toasters, hairdryers, printers, electric toothbrushes, dust busters, cell phone chargers, coffee grinders. For more information, see http://planetgreen.discovery.com/.

13. **Save money and reduce water usage.** Wash only full loads of laundry and save between 300-800 gallons of water a month. If you would like more information, see: http://planetgreen.discovery.com/.

14. **Set/buy a programmable thermostat** to adjust the heat or the air-conditioning automatically in the morning and at night to help you save money and not waste energy either (www.realsimple.com).

15. **Keep your dryer's lint filter clean.** A dirty lint filter uses 30% more energy to dry clothes. For more ideas, see www.realsimple.com/.

16. **Eating ice cream or frozen yogurt.** Get a cone instead of a cup and cut down on plastic utensils and paper or plastic cups (Oprah.com).

17. **Install a low-flow shower head.** When we take a shower, we use 5-7 gallons of water per minute. Change to a low-flow shower head and cut your water usage in half (from The Student Environment Action Guide—25 simple things we can do).

18. **Living Green, 12 Ways to Help the Planet** As a guest-blogger at "Prime Time: The Second Act Blog," Kim Masoner mentioned a lot of great ideas. I've included three of them in the following paragraph. See this site for more ideas: http://www.secondact.com/2011/07/living-green-12-things-you-can-do-to-help-the-planet/.

a. **Don't buy soda in a six pack with plastic rings.** If these rings find their way into the ocean, they harm animals. (Note from Sherri: I do the same, and if these plastic rings find their way into my house via a guest, I make sure to cut them up so sea life and animals don't get their heads or wings stuck in them.)

b. **Refill your printer cartridges** instead of buying new ones to reduce the amount of refuse in our landfills.

c. **Buy rechargeable batteries** instead of single-use batteries to reduce the amount of refuse in our landfills.

19. I've saved the most important suggestion to help the planet for last, and here it is: **eat less meat.** Jennise Davis mentioned earlier in this chapter that she has stopped consuming animals, and I'm sure many of you wondered how that decision on her part helps the planet. For the answer, here's Chip Giller of the environmental magazine, Grist.org:

a. Meat production takes a lot more energy and resources than growing vegetables or grains, and 18% of human-generated greenhouse gases come from the livestock industry.

b. You don't have to be a vegetarian to make a difference in this area: try skipping meat just one day a week. If every American had one meat-free day per week, it would reduce emissions as much as taking 8,000,000 cars off the roads.

My personal feelings about eating animals are well-documented in both *Windows of Opportunity* and *Raising Our Vibrations for the New Age*, and I'm not about to get on a soapbox and deliver a lecture about why we should be vegetarians. I'll save that for my next book, a vegetarian cookbook, that I'm currently working on with my niece, New York food blogger and photographer, Samantha Seeley.

# Chapter Eleven: Reducing Karmic Debt and Negative Energy

I realize that most of the readers of my books are Lightworkers, and I also know that the last people on Earth I need to give lessons to about karma are Lightworkers. However, *in the spirit of reducing future karmic debt and as an aid to help us avoid creating negative energy in the present*, a quick review is worth a few minutes of our time and attention.

Karma is a Universal Law that is based on action and reaction. It's very much a "cause and effect," reap what you sow type of law; and it works two ways:

1. If we do something against another person or nature, we will have to balance the negative energy we've created during our present incarnation (instant karma) or a future lifetime (karmic debt);

2. If we do nice things for people and our planet, we create positive energy, and this, too, will come back to us during our present incarnation or a future lifetime.

It follows then, that every waking moment of our lives we create energy, and whether that energy is positive or negative—well, that's completely up to us. We have a tremendous amount of responsibility. We also have the *ability* to control what we think, do, and say. The big plus here is that understanding the consequences of our actions helps us avoid the creation of additional negative energy or karmic debt. According to the GG:

GG: ***There is a force working within the universe called "karma." It is the law of cause and effect. It is the energy that you send forth—whether positive or negative—and it is the energy that you receive—either positive or negative. Cause and effect is a pretty simple concept. Any action will have a reaction . . . everything must balance in the end.***

There's another big benefit to understanding that we have karmic debts to repay from our previous and even our current lifetime.

Having this knowledge allows us to correctly process the unpleasant and even tragic things that happen in our lives. As the GG say,

GG: ***Not everything that happens is karmic, but with the exception of murder, suicide, and rape, most experiences are planned by the individual soul to help him[/her] progress. It could be that the soul is seeking a faster progression and has chosen to undergo a very tumultuous life . . . When bad things happen, there is most likely a plan behind it.***

We know that we plan the majority of what takes place in our lives, but there's that little thing called "freewill," which means that unplanned events can take place. Whether planned or unplanned, every choice we make during any given day has the potential to create additional karma. With each choice we make, we create positive or negative energy that becomes part of the karmic debt that we will pay or will be repaid during this lifetime (instant karma) or during a future incarnation. This is part of the process of being human, and being aware of how we acquire karmic debt serves an important purpose: we possess the wisdom that will guide us towards making better choices, which, in turn, will help us generate far less negative energy and create more positive energy over the course of our present incarnation.

Karma provides us with an opportunity to learn from past mistakes and grow; reincarnation is the vehicle that allows karma to play out. *We* have all the power and all the responsibility when it comes to deciding what karma we will deal with and what growth experiences we will include in a particular lifetime.

Let me repeat that statement because it is extremely important: **WE have all the power and all the responsibility when it comes to deciding what karma we will deal with and what growth experiences we will include in a particular lifetime.** This means that when something that we deem or perceive to be "bad" happens to us, it most likely happens because there is a lesson we want to learn or a debt we want to repay. Are we all on the same page? Great! Let's take a look at how we plan our lessons and experiences.

## Planning Our Lessons & Experiences

As we begin to prepare for an upcoming incarnation, we have a series of meetings with other entities: our Guides, counselors, Angels, and souls with whom we've incarnated in the past and/or those we will incarnate with in the upcoming lifetime that we're planning. Picture yourself sitting down with them at a conference table and taking out your laundry list of the things you want to accomplish. This list includes karmic debts you need or want to repay and other experiences you want to have for the growth of your soul. Visualize your upcoming life as the *Book of You* and imagine yourself outlining the chapters of your book as you and your planning committee create a lifetime of opportunities for you to accomplish everything that you want to get done.

Based on your goals, you'll choose your parents and siblings by searching for or creating a familial situation that will provide you with the best opportunities to complete the items on your spiritual To Do List. Your new parents, siblings, friends, acquaintances, and even the people who are going to "annoy the heck out of you" in the future will probably be sitting at the conference table with you as you plan your upcoming adventure.

We also have Guides and counselors present because sometimes we are extremely optimistic during the planning stages of a lifetime; so they are there to keep us from biting off more than we can chew. Keep in mind that while our Guides and counselors can advise us, ultimately, the choice of how much we will take on in any given lifetime is up to us because as individual entities, we are decisively in control of planning our incarnation.

It's a difficult thing, don't you think, to wrap our heads around the fact that we personally choose or decide to have unpleasant or negative experiences? When we're making our plans on the other side of the veil, we understand the meaning and purpose behind each experience we plan for ourselves; however, once we've reincarnated, we don't have that information at our fingertips. We are awake on the Other Side, and one of the goals we all have in common is to "wake up" on *this* side and realize when a lesson or window of opportunity for growth and learning is staring us in the face. The good news here is that we are firmly in charge of our future, and we can take steps to learn our lessons faster and create less negative energy.

To accomplish this, we have to do some *soul-searching*, something we'll get to . . . right now! The purpose of the following exercise is to help us recognize when we're in situations that could cause us to create negative karma/energy, identify the triggers that cause us to *lose our cool*, and figure out how we can change/modify our behavior when faced with similar situations in the future. No one is going to see this but you, so try to be as honest with yourself as possible. There will be other Spiritual Growth Checkpoints throughout this book.

**Spiritual Growth Checkpoint Exercise #1: Karma**

What types of situations are likely to cause you to "lose your cool" and create negative energy/karma?

______________________________________________

______________________________________________

______________________________________________

______________________________________________

When confronted with the above situations, what are the "triggers" that cause you to act or react with negativity?

______________________________________________

______________________________________________

Understanding that reacting with negativity will most likely create additional karmic debt that must be repaid at a later date, what steps can you take to defuse negative situations like the ones you described above?

What attitude and/or behavior modifications can you make when a similar situation/trigger occurs in the future?

______________________________________________

______________________________________________

______________________________________________

______________________________________________

______________________________________________

**Homework Assignment**

Keep a journal of your daily experiences for thirty days and record what happens each day that creates positive or negative energy. Use this insight to help you become aware of and avoid creating additional negative energy. This challenge will help you avoid creating negative karmic debt, accelerate spiritual growth, and generate more positive energy for yourself, those around you, and the planet.

# Chapter Twelve: Windows of Opportunity

## What Are Windows of Opportunity?

Remember earlier when we talked about sitting at a table and planning the things we wanted to learn and do when we came back into body? Well, let's say we decided that we're going to make "learning to communicate better" one of our goals for this lifetime. Once that decision was made, we then planned scenarios, situations or, as the GG calls them, "windows of opportunity," to provide us with chances to learn that lesson.

These *windows* are opportunities for growth and learning that we personally designed and created for ourselves while we were on the Other Side of the veil planning our present incarnation.

Remember earlier when we talked about visualizing the *Book of You*? That's your life plan, and each chapter is dedicated to a particular lesson or experience that you want to have. Into each chapter, we insert multiple scenarios or situations that we painstakingly construct to make sure that we have ample opportunities to reach each one of our life goals.

Now, to make my point—and I'm very sorry to do this to you—I have to bring up my love life. My first two husbands and countless boyfriends were basically the same guy—different color hair, different name, different build—but all *control freaks* in their own individual ways. I was continually having the same unsatisfying relationship over and over, and here's why.

I was living a life script, which is a series of windows of opportunity to learn lessons and grow. When we don't learn our lesson/s from the experience/s we have, we keep attracting similar ones until we finally "get it." Life scripts are messages from the universe—messages from ourselves to wake the heck up, to open our eyes, and to start recognizing what's going on in our lives.

We all have windows of opportunity built into our lives. Here's a little something from the GG on this subject:

GG: ***Recognize earlier on the life scripts that keep [you] in the cycle of karma and the windows of opportunity that will get you out of that cycle . . . Recognize that a particular situation is something you are here to work on, and you will take the steps through those windows much sooner to learn a particular lesson.***

***We should look at the big picture by looking for script-like occurrences and evaluating what's happening with individual situations to see if there is a window of opportunity. If there is and we go for it, we will accelerate learning.***

***As we start to do this, we will gain experience in doing so. This means we will work less hard when it comes to our lessons because we will recognize them earlier.***

And this is a perfect segue into what we need to talk about next—looking for windows of opportunity.

**Why Look for Windows of Opportunity?**

Let's go back to my love life for a minute. Had I spotted my life script of getting involved with controlling men earlier, I would have saved myself *and* a couple of husbands and boyfriends some unhappy relationships and a whole lot of drama and pain. I also would have learned my lessons faster, which would have *accelerated* my spiritual growth by leaving me free to work on other items on my To Do List.

So each time we learn a lesson or complete an experience on our To Do List for this lifetime, we have more time to work on other items on our list. And the more we accomplish, the more rapidly we mature spiritually.

In case you're wondering why I was so attracted to controlling men, it's because I needed to learn to stand up for myself and communicate my feelings. Taking crap for years and then storming out of the relationship did *not* move me forward spiritually. To make progress and start *going through windows* instead of *attracting more of them*, I had to change the only two things I could change: my behavior and my attitude during life-script situations.

Now here's the stickler when it comes to windows. As we miss one window and go on to another, the windows become increasingly more difficult and dramatic. We set ourselves up for this because when we're on the Other Side figuring out our windows, we can sometimes be just a little bit *cocky*. We create some "slap you in your face" ways to wake ourselves up, figuring it will help us learn the lesson the first time we're presented with a window. We expect to avoid life scripts and the need for dramatic situations, but it doesn't usually happen that way.

Once we have an understanding of windows under our belts, our new goal is to learn how to spot our windows closer to the ground floor instead of in the penthouse. As we develop this skill, we'll learn our lessons with less drama and pain, *and* we'll accelerate our spiritual growth because we will be able to move on to other lessons and experiences more quickly.

To summarize, if the same type of situation keeps occurring in your life, that's a clear message that you should examine how you dealt with it in the past and then change your behavior/reaction/attitude. Altering how you dealt with similar situations will eventually enable you to go through the window and stop the pattern from continuing to repeat in the future.

Okay, we know what a window is and why we want to look for them, so let's talk next about how to spot them.

## Spotting Windows

I've been "window watching" for several years now, and I can tell you this: it gets easier and easier to spot them as you go along. **It's a skill** that we can all develop over time. A good sign that we've got an open window in front of us is when something that's going on in our lives is a repeat of a similar situation we've already lived through once or twice, or maybe even three or four times. This is how we look for patterns and life scripts, which again are essentially a series of windows of opportunity that we've set in motion to make sure we learn a particular lesson.

So where are these windows? They are everywhere—at home, at work, even at the grocery store. Any place you are, there could be a window. And I'm going to say this again because it's so important: the best way to find our windows is to examine our lives and look for patterns because patterns scream to us that we're missing windows. Once we recognize a pattern/life script, we know we've missed windows of opportunity to learn something that's very important to us on a soul level. There are three steps we can take to correct this oversight, but again, we have to be brutally honest with ourselves, or we're wasting our time.

**Step #1: Examine your past.**

- If you draw similar situations to yourself, the universe is trying to get your attention.
- If you continue to draw the same type of person to you, the universe is sending you a message.
- If you have similar disagreements with people over and over, and you think, "What's wrong with all these people?" they might be providing you with windows of opportunity.

**Step #2: Connect the past with the present.**

- Pay attention to what's happening in the present; be aware of what's happening in your life today.
- Is there a similarity between situations you find yourself in now and what you've been through in the past?
- Comparing the present to the past will help you identify patterns and life scripts.
- If nothing stands out for you, ask your family and friends.
    - Often the people we are closest to will be able to see patterns and life scripts that we miss.
    - Ask them if they have noticed any patterns or scripts in your life.
    - They will tell you right away!!

**Step #3: Devise a plan of action for future windows.**

- Review your behavior and reactions to past situations that make up your life script.
- Determine changes that you can make the next time a similar situation occurs.
- Continue making changes to your attitude, behavior, and reactions until this type of situation stops presenting itself.

Enough talk! It's time for action! You will find Spiritual Growth Checkpoint Exercises 2, 3, and 4 in this chapter, and more are coming up in the next chapter. These are designed to help you get started spotting patterns and life scripts in your life today. Please remember that honesty is of the utmost importance when it comes to revealing the patterns and life scripts that have previously gone unnoticed.

**Spiritual Growth Checkpoint Exercise #2: Windows of Opportunity**

Review difficult or challenging situations that you've experienced in the past with friends, family members, and/or co-workers.

- What underlying theme, topic, or subject is connected to these situations?
- How did you react during and after these situations?
- What lesson are you trying to learn from this life script or series of windows of opportunity?
- Are you experiencing something similar now?
- What changes in your own attitude or behavior are necessary to learn this lesson?

________________________________________

________________________________________

________________________________________

________________________________________

________________________________________

________________________________________

________________________________________

________________________________________

**Spiritual Growth Checkpoint Exercise #3: Relationships**

Review romantic relationships and friendships to determine if you tend to be attracted to the same personality type, and if so, describe the type.

- Are you currently involved with someone who exhibits these traits?
- What lesson are you trying to learn from people who exhibit these characteristics?
- What changes in your own attitude or behavior are necessary to learn this lesson?

______________________________________________

______________________________________________

______________________________________________

______________________________________________

______________________________________________

______________________________________________

______________________________________________

**Spiritual Growth Checkpoint Exercise #4: Behavior Modification**

Continually prepare yourself to walk through windows by reviewing your behavior, attitudes, and reactions to past and present situations that make up a life script. Determine what changes you can make the next time a similar window opens, and you'll be ready to go through it and cross that lesson off your list.

- Is there a topic(s) of conversation or a behavior of yours that promotes similar disagreements with multiple friends, family members, co-workers, or even strangers on the street or at the supermarket?
- Can you connect these situations to an underlying theme, topic, or subject?
- What message could people be trying to give you when they disagree with you or your behavior?

- What changes can you make to get the message and learn the lesson?

_______________________________________________

_______________________________________________

_______________________________________________

_______________________________________________

_______________________________________________

_______________________________________________

_______________________________________________

# Chapter Thirteen: Relationship Villains

## What Are Relationship Villains?

We're not in this world alone. We're surrounded by entities who are here to help us accomplish our goals—all of whom were at that planning table when we decided what we wanted to learn and accomplish during this lifetime.

Let me throw this out to you the way the Guide Group first gave it to me: "What if the people who annoy us the most, the people we don't like, the people who irritate the heck out of us or even cause us trouble are actually our closest, most beloved, universal friends?"

These friends are here to help us—and we help them, too—by playing the roles of our mothers, fathers, sisters, brothers, husbands, wives, friends, co-workers, even strangers we pass on the street or meet at mall, grocery store, and even the Department of Motor Vehicles. And sometimes these entities take on what the GG calls the "Relationship Villain role." Rather than paraphrase for the GG, here's what they initially dictated on this subject:

GG: ***We sit and plan our lives here on Earth. We are here with many entities, all of whom play many different roles in our many lifetimes, and our point today is that it is those who love us the most who will play the role of the villain. This is because they love us enough to want to make sure that we accomplish what we wish to accomplish for ourselves—even when it means being perceived as the bad guy.***

***The "villains" in your life, most of the time, are really your most amazing friends because they are sacrificing so that you can learn and grow. Sometimes it seems as though we truly dislike someone, but that entity, in truth, could be one of your most beloved friends outside of this incarnation--someone who loves you enough to do you a big favor.***

What the GG are saying is that when people do what we perceive to be mean, unkind, annoying, or rude things to us, they may well be doing us a favor by opening up a window of opportunity. Souls that are our best friends when we're on the Other Side are the ones most likely to put on the black hat and play the role of villain to help cross off an important lesson on our "Must Learn List" for this incarnation. Why? Because anyone can play the hero, but it takes someone who really cares about helping us grow and achieve our goals to play the villain role. And to open a window, we need a catalyst. Relationship villains are *catalysts* for windows of opportunity.

**Who Are Relationship Villains?**

The bottom line is that relationship villains can be anyone and everywhere. Look for them in romantic relationships, family relationships, and work relationships. They will also turn up at school, the grocery store, the airport, the DMV, and anywhere you happen to be. They can be someone you have an on-going relationship with or someone you interact with just once or twice. When you learn the lesson, your interactions with your Relationship Villain will become much more palatable. This is usually the case when the villain is a family member, or your relationship may end because your mission together is over—as often happens with friends.

**How Can I Spot My Relationship Villains?**

To help *me* fully comprehend how relationship villains accelerate spiritual growth, the GG asked me to do a review of my past romantic relationships. Now *that* was a homework assignment I was not thrilled about because I knew it was going to be a painful walk down memory lane, but it had to be done. Once I did it, I was able to recognize distinct patterns of behavior on my part that needed to change and then start moving forward by figuring out what steps I needed to take to end the pattern/life script. After following the GG's advice and taking the time to put this information into action, I've learned many lessons, and I was able to quit my second job as a drama queen starring in my own personal soap opera. I've done it. I'm still doing it, and you can do it, too.

Since relationship villains are catalysts for opening windows of opportunity throughout our lives, we look for them the same we look for windows of opportunity—by searching for patterns and life scripts. To spot relationship villains in your life at the present time, consider the following:

- Are you involved in on-going arguments or unpleasant situations that are continually caused by the same person? If *yes*, that person is probably a Relationship Villain working very hard to help you learn a lesson. Consider the circumstances and look for patterns to help you figure out your lesson.
- If you've been involved in a car accident, or someone *does you wrong* at work, it is most likely a Relationship Villain providing you with a window of opportunity for growth. How you react to the situation will dictate whether you go through the window or attract a similar situation again in the future. If you've had comparable experiences in the past, reacting differently this time may help you put an end to this particular life script.

**Spotting Past Relationship Villains (AND Keeping Them Out of Our Future)**

Sit down and do a mini-life review by carefully and honestly looking at situations surrounding people you feel have *done you wrong*—those in your life that you find particularly annoying, those you feel or know have brought upset and tragedy into your life, and even folks that you just plain don't like.

Carefully review the circumstances around your interaction/s with them and ask yourself these questions:

- Did I learn anything from my experience with this person?
- Would things have been different for me if I had handled the situation differently?

You may find that the people *you think* did you wrong actually made things better for you in the long run. I know I did. Here are Spiritual Growth Checkpoint Exercises #5 and 6 to help you get started identifying your relationship villains right away. This will also help you identify patterns and life scripts to enable you to spread some positive energy within these relationships.

**Spiritual Growth Checkpoint Exercise #5: Relationship Villains**

1) Do a mini-life review and examine situations surrounding people you feel have *done you wrong* and those in your life that you find particularly annoying or challenging. List a few below.

______________________________________________

______________________________________________

______________________________________________

______________________________________________

______________________________________________

______________________________________________

______________________________________________

2) Carefully review the circumstances around your interaction/s with them and ask yourself these questions:

a. Did I learn anything from my experience with this person?

b. Is there more than one way to look at what transacted between the two of us?

c. Would things have been different for me if I had handled the situation differently?

d. How could I have acted and reacted differently (attitude/behavior), and what effect would a change on my part have had on the situation/interaction?

______________________________________________

______________________________________________

______________________________________________

______________________________________________

______________________________________________

______________________________________________

______________________________________________

3) List your *hot buttons*—the things that set you off on an everyday basis; for example, people who pull out in front of you on the highway, people who bang into your cart at the supermarket, or the person who doesn't refill the copy paper.

a. How do react when someone presses one of your *hot buttons*?

b. What changes you can make in your behavior to diffuse these types of situations?

c. What will happen if you change your behavior and cool your *hot buttons*?

## Spiritual Growth Checkpoint Exercise #6: Generating Positive Energy

When you find yourself in a situation where negativity and discord are present, look for ways to sprinkle positive energy into the mix by communicating your feelings to the other person/s in a non-judgmental manner. Finding out the other person's point of view will help you determine behavior/attitude changes that will help you keep a negative pattern from repeating in the future. What are some of the ways that you can do this?

═✦═

If we can accept our role in planning the things that happen to us, like car accidents, for example, we'll be that much more awake when it comes to being on the lookout for our windows of opportunity. Taking responsibility for what happens to us will help us expedite our growth because we'll forgive ourselves and others faster, especially the relationship villains that cause unpleasant situations/circumstances and sometimes even tragic events to happen in our lives. We'll be free to move forward.

# SECTION FIVE

# MAINTAINING BALANCE AND WELL-BEING

# Chapter Fourteen: Advice from a Spiritual Wellness and Soul Coach

In an earlier chapter, I first mentioned my dear friend and psychic medium Mitchell Osborn, who is also a Spiritual Wellness Coach. His website is www.intuitivemessenger.org. There are many qualities I admire about Mitchell, and I particularly love that he uses his intuitive, psychic and mediumistic abilities as a bridge to deliver messages from Spirit. More importantly, I admire the way he uses his gifts to help his clients move forward *on their own.* I asked Mitchell if he would share his journey and some spiritual wellness and communication tips with us, and he has done so much more. I am honored to share the following special guest chapter, which I know you will love as much as I do. Here's Mitchell.

**My Search for Truth by Mitchell Osborn**

Many years ago, when my journey for TRUTH started, I reluctantly went to a chiropractor. My neck was really hurting me. I was doing mini-triathlons and teaching a lot of group fitness classes. Seeing a chiropractor was a *last resort* thing since I didn't grow up with an understanding of what a chiropractor does. I look back now and wonder what took me so long to make that appointment.

One of the first things my chiropractor said at the end of our adjustment was, "I hope I don't have to see you again."

She must have read my face and mind because she quickly explained, "If you are healthy and doing the things you are supposed to be doing, you will stay in alignment and won't need to see me."

This simple but profound lesson continued with me in my life as a personal trainer and especially as an Intuitive Messenger. I truly want my clients to stay in alignment with Source so they don't have to see me again. My intention is to teach them to fish and not just give them a fish.

When I work with clients in sessions, I always encourage them to do the work on their own—to get in touch with Spirit, their Higher Self or listen to their gut-level intuition. And they usually walk away with homework. I give them a structure of Five Dimensions of Wellness to focus on, using the acronym S.P.I.E.S (Social, Physical, Intellectual, Emotional and the umbrella of all, Spiritual.)

As I move energetically through five dimensions during a session, I use the imagery of a room or place that is familiar to me. I encourage clients to do the same without limiting them by telling them how I do it; instead, I give them the opportunity to use the Five Dimensions of Wellness structure that follows until they feel comfortable with their own imagery for "journeying."

**Mitchell's Five Dimensions of Wellness Preparation**

**To start working on balancing your Five Dimensions of Wellness, find a quiet place to meditate and journey.**

Like most, I recommend that you sit upright in a comfortable chair with your feet flat on the ground, but this is not always necessary. So many get hung up on how everyone else does it that it stifles their growth with worries of whether or not they are doing it correctly. Start with someone's structure and then allow your Higher Self to guide you to what works best for you. It will come so naturally—just trust it.

**Once you have your quiet place prepared, find a time of day that you won't be interrupted.**

Many teachers encourage doing the journey the same place and same time of day. I tried this and got frustrated when I couldn't always do it at the same time and place. That is why I again stress ***do what works for you***. Turn off your phone or move it to another room if you choose to leave it on vibrate—often you can still feel that vibration if it's near you.

**Begin your journey by allowing your eyes to close and focusing inward and on your breath**.

Once you feel relaxed and *present*, move to the Area of Wellness you choose or feel the need to experience. I do recommend going to the Spiritual Dimension last if you are doing a complete evaluation/assessment of yourself and going through all five dimensions. Have a pad of paper and pen near you, or your iPad, recorder or laptop. Once again, DO WHAT WORKS FOR YOU.

**Beginning the Journey**

*You might want to record this first, so you don't have to try to journey and read directions simultaneously.*

**Once you are quiet, relaxed, present and ready to journey, imagine a long hallway with one door at the end.**

- Walk down the hallway to the locked door and take out the key that is always with you and only you! With each step know you are going deeper into a mental state of journeying.
- Open the door and walk into the Wellness room. Close and lock the door behind you. This ritual sets you up to journey more quickly and successfully each time by alerting your Higher Self and all those who assist you from the Other Side that you are *on your way*.
- The room is white with mostly all white features and equipment. To your right is a desk with a beautiful white computer on it. On both sides of the desk are bookshelves filled with volumes of books with no writing on the binders.
- Straight ahead is a warm, inviting, comfortable massage therapy table with a giant screen TV behind it. Off to your left is a bench facing a window with the curtains drawn.
- The entire room is filled with light but not bright.

**Ending the Journey**

After visiting the Wellness Dimension/s of your choice, exit the room in reverse order of the way you entered.

- Walk to the door where you entered the room. Use your key to unlock it.

- Turn around one more time and give thanks for what you learned on your journey there. Breathe in your knowing. Smile.
- Open the door. Walk into the hallway. Turn and lock the door behind you.
- Walk slowly down the hallway with each step taking you back to physicality more and more enlightened, energized, and grateful.

**Visiting the Wellness Dimensions**

Now that you know the procedures to begin and end your visitations to the five dimensions, let's get started.

**Social Wellness Dimension**

- To experience the Social Wellness Dimension, energetically move through this light-filled wellness room to the desk on your right and have a seat in front of the computer. Log in to your Facebook account or envision a fake one if you don't have a real Facebook account or have not used this network before. Avoid getting hung up on how to do it. Just set your intention.
- We use the imagery of a Facebook account to see who is in your social network and what they are saying and projecting in life. If you aren't familiar with Facebook, then see an album with all your social contacts and information about your interactions with each one. You have to be realistic and willing to "weed your social garden" when led to do so.
- Look at posts on the screen/information in the album. See who projects positivity and who doesn't. Take or make notes. Ask silently or verbally for Spirit to show you what you need to see on the screen/in the album in order to help raise your vibration in the dimension of Social Wellness.
- What you need to know will appear. Make notes. This is where you will find guidance.
- If you have a specific question about this dimension, ASK for guidance and then see what appears on the screen/in the album. If there is ONE thing I can say that will help the

most, it is "ASK questions of your team" and listen and look for answers. So many forget to ask while life is going on around them.

**Physical Wellness Dimension**

- To experience the Physical Wellness Dimension, walk into this well-lighted wellness room knowing YOUR body is covered with a sheet and lying on the therapy table straight ahead.
- From a comfortable distance, objectively scan your body lying there. See if there is dis-ease or illness.
- You may know this intuitively and/or receive clues and guidance on the TV screen behind the table. You may see x-rays, pictures or simple instructions.
- After you know or have a feeling about what is going on in your body, ask what to DO to remedy the situation.
- Allow the information to come to you naturally and easily. Make notes.

**Intellectual Wellness Dimension**

- To experience the Intellectual Wellness Dimension, walk this well-lighted wellness room and go directly to the bookshelves on the left of the desk for insights into past and present situations and/or to the bookshelves on the right for information or guidance on the future.
- Stand in front of the shelves and trust you will select the correct book. Avoid thinking too much at all.
- Just grab a book and sit at the desk.
- Open anywhere and let the words or pictures on the page envelop you with the knowing of what you need to hear, see, feel, taste and know.
- Make notes. And remember to ASK questions, either silently or aloud.

**Emotional Wellness Dimension**

- To experience the Emotional Wellness Dimension, walk into this well-lighted wellness room.

- Sit at the desk and pull out the middle drawer.
- Inside is a beautiful heart-shaped box. Open it to find pastel-colored candy hearts. You know the kind—the ones with little messages on them.
- Present your emotional quandaries. Ask Spirit a question and dive into the drawer to grab one heart.
- Read the message. Take notes.
- Ask more questions and draw/select more hearts if needed.
- Write down everything you get. It all can have a wonderful effect on you later when you are back to the daily grind.

**Spiritual Wellness Dimension**

***IMPORTANT: If you only have time to visit one wellness dimension, this one is the "umbrella that encompasses all."***

- To experience the Spiritual Wellness Dimension, walk into well-lighted wellness room and go directly to the bench facing the window on the left side of the room.
- As you take your seat on the bench, ask for a guide, angel, gatekeeper or deceased relative to come and sit by you.
- Wait for that being/spirit to come. You must *ask* because it won't intrude.
- If you don't know who to ask for, tell Spirit to send someone who can help you. Then wait to see who it will be.
- Get a good sense of the being/spirit sitting by you. Energetically hold its hand or lean on it.
- Allow the window to open to a scene that will show you your journey in physical life. Your companion is there to explain what it is you are seeing.
- All you have to do is ask. It is lovingly there to help you along this amazing experience called LIFE.
- When your time with the being is finished, thank it and make a few notes.

Thank you, Mitchell!

What a treat! A mini-workshop! Mitchell's advice to ***not get all hung up on doing things other people's ways*** is very important. I've already shared that I've wasted a fair amount of time trying to do so myself. There is no right or wrong way to work with Spirit. There is simply your way and my way and others' ways.

# Chapter Fifteen: Meditating & Working with Crystals and Stones

## Five Great Reasons to Use Crystals During Meditation

There are a multitude of reasons to include crystals and stones in our meditation practice—all of which are directly related to mingling their energies and vibrations with our own, which ultimately facilitates communication with Spirit. We're all drawn or attracted to different crystals at different times of our lives, and here are five great reasons to incorporate crystals and stones into our daily meditation practice:

1. to deepen our meditation practice and enhance visualization;
2. to assist communication with our Higher Self, Guides, and Angels;
3. to balance mind, body and Spirit;
4. to heal our body, mind and soul; and
5. to calm the mind and soothe the Spirit.

As we meditate, we can hold a particular crystal or stone or a combination of crystals and stones in our hand/s to assist us in communicating with Spirit to promote healing or to balance one or more of our chakras (see Section Six for an in-depth look at chakras). We can also focus our attention directly on one particular crystal or stone in order to tune into its individual energy frequency and receive assistance with healing, balancing, communication and visualization. And, of course, we can wear crystal and stone jewelry to drink in and absorb their wonderful energies during meditation and all day long.

How do we know which crystal or stone to meditate with or wear? We trust that little voice inside of us, listen to our gut, and reach for the crystals and stones that call out to us. We choose the ones that feel right to us. A little further down in this chapter, you'll find suggestions on how to choose crystals and stones along with a list of which crystals/stones work well with regard to balancing our individual chakras. In Section Six, you'll find lots of information regarding the effects of various colors on our bodies.

Now I have a surprise for you. I am very excited to introduce you to my good friend, Paige Hall-Ferraro. See her website at www.paigehallferraro.com. Paige is a psychic, medium, Reiki Master, *and* a crystal healer. Among her many workshops are chakra balancing and psychic development; and I was overjoyed when she agreed to write a "guest chapter" for this section. She's gone above and beyond and also included a special meditation that she uses to receive messages from the crystal kingdom. I will not keep you waiting any longer . . . here's Paige.

**Loving Insights About Crystals by Paige Hall Ferraro**

Crystals are so much more than a pretty or decorative piece of jewelry. When we work lovingly with crystal energy, we create a partnership with the crystal kingdom that is nothing less than magical. Crystals have the amazing potential to raise our vibrations, balance our energy field, and assist in healing ailments on the physical, emotional and spiritual levels. There really is no limit as to how crystals can assist us. All we need to do is choose a crystal that calls to us, cleanse it properly, and then program it with a purpose for our highest good. Once this is done, our crystal becomes a faithful friend and will be ready to take care of us whenever we call upon it.

My mother, Terrie Reichwein, was a well-known clairvoyant and medium, who also worked with crystals. As a girl, I was always drawn to shimmering rocks and sea shells, so I was especially intrigued when she would use crystals in meditation. She explained to me the various properties of the crystals she worked with the most and gifted me with my very first crystal over thirty years ago: a beautiful rose quartz that I still have to this day! Over the years, my crystals have traveled with me to various parts of the world, and I truly believe that they chose me, instead of the other way around.

Here's something interesting: each of my clear quartz clusters has grown new crystal formations. When I first began to notice this happening, I confess that I thought maybe I was going crazy, but after comparing photos that were taken over a period of twelve months, I realized that I wasn't going crazy at all—my crystals *were growing*! This discovery encouraged me to pay even closer attention to the messages my crystals were telling me. The most important and powerful message the crystals have for us is that it's time to raise our vibrations higher, so we are in alignment with our Higher Self, the planet and each other as we embrace the most important shift of ages.

My lifelong passion and admiration for crystals is utilized every day in my career as a Lightworker. I encourage others to incorporate crystals into their daily lives by educating them about the healing properties, vibration and uses of crystals. As a crystal healer, I formulate elixirs and aura sprays of all kinds made with crystals, and I teach others how to use a crystal grid for spiritual protection, manifestation, and as a means of bringing love into one's life. Something new that I've been working with is the infusion of crystal energy and healing with Reiki treatments.

All of the things I just mentioned are important and valuable; however, I feel that the best and truly the most effective crystal healing technique we have for raising our vibrations to heal ourselves, each other and the planet is to *meditate with crystals*. I meditate on a regular basis with such crystals as clear quartz, amethyst, rose quartz or celestite because these crystals have a very high vibration and activate the higher chakras. However, I encourage you to choose the crystal/s that you have come to love. When we meditate with crystals, we can reach the depths of our Higher Self, receive guidance from the crystal kingdom, and magnify our personal energy. Not only does crystal meditation allow more peace, clarity and well-being into our daily lives; it also raises our energetic vibration, which benefits us and the planet.

Before we get to the meditation, let's talk about cleansing and programming our crystals and stones.

## Choosing Crystals and Stones

Expect the crystals and stones that are right for you to find their way into your life. Choosing crystals and stones isn't rocket-science. It's based on our feelings and gut reactions when we see or pick up a crystal/stone. You'll develop a *feel* for choosing crystals/stones. To help you get started, here's some advice from Paige that is followed by some advice from me.

### Suggestions for Starting Your Crystal and/or Stone Collection

1. Always choose stones that you are personally drawn/attracted to.
2. To build a crystal collection that you can use for chakra balancing, select ones in these colors: clear, violet, indigo, purple, blue, green, pink, yellow, orange, red and black.
3. Good "starter" stones for your collection are clear quartz, amethyst, and pink (rose) quartz—they are very powerful and will help connect you to Spirit.
4. If you are attracted to the color, shape, or texture of a crystal, then simply let that be your guide and let go of the reason "why" for now. Crystals hold a vibration and interact with our human energy field, so they can be very beneficial for bringing the body, mind and Spirit back into balance. You can hold a crystal in your hand and instantly notice if you feel calm, happy and peaceful.
5. On the flip side, if you feel uncomfortable holding it, then it probably isn't the right one for you at this time.

I also teach my students and clients how to finger dowse. Since our physical body rarely lies to us, I find this to be a reliable technique to discover crystals and stones that want to work with us. So, if you tend to doubt your inner guidance, give this simple method a try.

Begin by looping your thumb and finger

together. Then slip your other thumb and finger through the loop and close them as shown in the photo (http://spiritualdeepdish.com/2008/01/).

Hold this position over the crystal you are considering and ask if this one is beneficial for you.

Pull steadily.

If the loop breaks, the answer is NO.

If the loop holds, the answer is YES.

Lastly, whenever I need a crystal for something specific, I begin by stating an intention like this one: "I am now guided to the exact crystal I need for (fill in the blank)." The universe will attract the exact crystal we need for our highest good. Happy crystal shopping!

### Sherri's Advice for Selecting Crystals

First things first! Prior to working with crystals and stones, we must first acquire them. The quest to choose appropriate stones is a very personal journey. During a psychic development course, my teacher, Cyndi, taught us the following process, with the *caveat* that it is often the crystal that does the choosing, not the other way around! I've used this method for twenty-five years:

- Pick up a crystal or stone that attracts you.
- Place it in your left hand (or non-dominant/receiver hand).
- Loosely close your fingers around it in a relaxed fist.
- Extend your arm in front of you.
- Tune into, listen to, and feel the crystal/stone in your hand.

I always select crystals/stones that vibrate in my hand and/or make me feel happy, peaceful, and positive. Often I feel a great sense of camaraderie when I pick up a crystal that I'm attracted to—as if we've been friends for eons.

Crystals are light and crystals are energy. Like human beings, each one is an individual and deserves to be treated with respect. When you're considering a crystal/stone and holding it in your left hand, open your heart and mind to allow communication to flow between the two of you. Also, as Katrina Raphael states in her *Crystal Enlightenment* series of books, "Drop any pre-conceived notions, expectations, or fears . . . allow the inner mind to receive subtle impressions."

One last piece of advice: don't get all caught up in wondering if you're making the right choice. You'll know when a crystal/stone is right for you. Listen to your gut (aka your Higher Self), and you will always make the correct choice.

══✦══

**Paige's Advice for Cleansing Crystals/Stones**

"When and why do I cleanse my crystals?" you might ask.

I cleanse my crystals after each healing session with an individual, before I gift them to anyone else, and whenever I sense that they need it. Crystals hold the vibrations or energies of everyone who comes in contact with them. Just as humans do, crystals also absorb the energy from their surroundings, so it makes sense to cleanse our crystals on a regular basis. Just as we need to clear our energy from lower vibrations, we need to do the same for our crystal friends.

There are various methods for cleansing crystals. Keep in mind that we need to be careful with soft or fragile crystals. If you are just getting started on your crystal journey and are unsure if your crystal is too fragile to cleanse with filtered water, I recommend simply placing it in a bowl of brown rice and/or leaving it in the sun or under the moonlight for at least 12-24 hours. I especially recommend these methods for raw or naturally formed crystals, such as clusters.

However, if you are cleansing a tumbled (polished) crystal or stone, you can simply hold it under filtered water or cleanse it in the ocean. Then leave it in the sun or under the moonlight afterwards. Another simple cleansing method is to visualize your crystal in a cocoon of cleansing white light and washing away any negative/lower energies that it may have absorbed. Each of these methods will cleanse and recharge your crystals, and they will be ready to assist you with their renewed energy.

**Paige's Directions for Programming Crystals/Stones**

When you bring home a new crystal, you'll want to program it or *give it a job to do*. Once your crystal has been cleansed, dedicate a purpose for its use. Even if you have researched the specific properties of the crystal you have acquired, you must still set an intention for it, for that is how it will best be of service for you.

For example, if you want to program a rose quartz crystal, you might set an intention such as *I now dedicate this rose quartz for the highest good of all. May this crystal be used to attract unconditional love into my life. This rose quartz is programmed in love, light and clarity. And so it is.* Simultaneously, you might wish to imagine a radiant white light surrounding it or hold it in front of the flame of a rose-scented candle.

Be specific with your intention and follow your inner guidance. If you are seeking prosperity or healing, then state so precisely. Once your crystal is programmed or attuned, it should be placed in an area where you will see it often or kept next to your bed or in a pocket. Please hold your crystal often and repeat your intention several times until you feel or sense that it has been absorbed.

Lastly, please store your crystals gently, even the polished stones. The better you care for your crystal friends, the happier they will be, and their vibration will extend even further than you can imagine!

**Paige's Crystal Meditation Exercise**

Are you ready to try meditating with crystals? Here's the crystal meditation that I practice several times a week. For this specific meditation, I suggest using a high-vibration crystal, such as clear quartz, amethyst, elestial, celestite, blue moonstone, petalite, or Lemurian seed.

- Find some peaceful music for your meditation. I always recommend this because crystals can actually absorb and hold the etheric message of the music you listen to as you work with your crystal/s; therefore, if you meditate with that crystal often, it will raise your vibration even higher.

- Set your intention for the meditation with love. When we meditate, it's so important to let go and allow ourselves to be open to simply being one with our crystal. A positive intention that I use often is to ask my crystal to *Please show me what I need to know for the highest and best of all concerned and help me to feel, see, or hear any messages that you have to share.*

- Sit comfortably in a dimly lit room where you won't be disturbed. Lighting a candle creates a relaxing atmosphere and is helpful when meditating with crystals.

- With your music turned on, place your crystal loosely in your hand and take several deep breaths. Continue to breathe gently until you are relaxed.

- When you are relaxed, you can open your eyes and look deeply into your crystal. Simply gaze at your crystal and all its angles and imagine yourself inside the crystal and what that might feel like to you.

- When you have immersed all of your senses with your crystal, continue to breathe gently and close your eyes. Allow the peace and amazement you experienced with your crystal to take you into a deep, relaxed state of being.

- Continue to breathe gently with your crystal held loosely in your hand. Imagine this crystal is surrounding your entire being until you feel one with the crystal. You might notice feelings of peace and serenity or receive a message of some kind from the crystal. Perhaps it will guide you to be on a better diet, or you may see certain colors; whatever it is, simply notice and keep it in your memory.

- You might feel a little tingly from the crystal's vibration—just continue breathing and being one with your crystal.

- (Initially, suggested meditation time is 15 minutes. You may increase this time later if you choose.) When you are ready to end the meditation, you can open your eyes and bring your focus back to your crystal. Most likely, you will feel peaceful, yet energized. Take your hands away from the crystal now to disconnect from its energy.

- Be sure to take a moment to thank your crystal for its assistance. Then place the crystal on the floor or table next to you.
- Stand up and stretch.

You have now completed your crystal meditation connection! I recommend recording in your journal anything you may have felt, heard or seen during your meditation. Crystals will change over time the more they are used, and you will find that your relationship with your crystals and stones will become more intimate each time you meditate with them.

The more you meditate with crystals and stones, the more comfortable you'll become with them, and I know that you'll come to love getting to know and working with the crystal kingdom as much as Paige and I do. And before we move on to Section Six, many thanks to Paige for sharing her crystal expertise with us in a way that's easy to understand and easily put into action.

# SECTION SIX

# CHAKRAS AND CHAKRA BALANCING

**Overview**

Do you want to be healthy and happy and vibrate at the highest level possible? Me, too! Balancing our chakras will help us achieve these goals and more because when our chakras are open and balanced, it's easier for us to communicate with Spirit. In this section, we're going to explore the following:

- our auras and where they're located;
- our chakras, their anatomy and function and where they're located;
- chakra balancing as a road to better health;
- an exercise to practice seeing auras; and two chakra balancing meditations that will raise our vibrational levels as well. (The chakra balancing meditations are on the CD included with this book.)

# Chapter Sixteen: Our Aura

## Defining an Aura

Before we can talk about our chakras, we need to first understand what an aura is because our seven main chakras, which we are going to talk about in great depth, are located inside our aura.

*Aura* is a Latin word meaning "light" or "glow of light." Our auras are multi-layered energy fields that surround our bodies. Some people can see them, and there's a process called Kirlian photography where photos can be taken of our auras. By looking at the dark or weak spots in our aura, energy workers can tell where dis-ease is beginning long before it starts to manifest physically. Okay, we're going to get "science-y" for a minute.

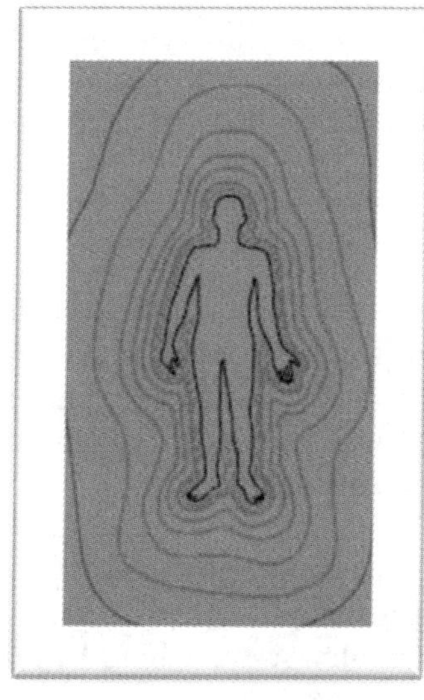

It's possible to see our auras because they're made up of electromagnetic energy, which surrounds and penetrates all living things. Modern science recognizes the existence of electromagnetic energy, and the "electromagnetic spectrum" is the name that scientists use when they want to talk about different kinds of energy "as a group." The source of this drawing is www.creativespirit.com/aurabook.html.

Part of the electromagnetic spectrum is the light we get from a light bulb, radio waves, and microwaves. Infrared light is also part of this group, and scientists say that because our skin emits infrared light, we can be seen in the dark with night vision goggles. Knowing that our bodies give off energy in the form of light and that scientists agree we can see this energy, it's suddenly not so far-fetched to believe that auras exist and that some people can see them.

Our auras have twelve layers. Each auric layer relates to the physical, mental, emotional and spiritual aspects of our bodies, and each of the twelve layers vibrates at a specific energy frequency. The higher vibrating energy frequencies interface with our spiritual needs, and the lower vibrating frequencies interface with our material or physical needs.

All the auric layers function interactively with our body, the energy points within our body, and our chakras. Like our chakras, our auras vibrate at certain color frequencies, and both are quite colorful. The colors in our auras change and vary according to our physical, mental, emotional and spiritual condition, which means that *the colors of our aura change, depending on our thoughts and feelings and how we are feeling physically.* This is how someone who reads auras and chakras can tell how a person is physically or mentally. They can tell by the intensity level of the colors and can spot blockages which appear as dark spots in the aura. What follows is a description of the layers and the colors associated with each layer, but you don't need to be an expert on them or memorize them in order to balance your chakras.

**Exercise to Practice Seeing Auras**

I've not yet seen anyone's auric colors, but even as a child, I could see a kind of white/silver glow around people, animals, and even plants. I know from researching auras and also from Reiki Master and Intuitive Medium, Shelly Wilson, that what I see is called the etheric aura, which is a white outline around the body.

In preparation for writing this section, I read many books and looked at numerous websites for ways to learn how to see auras. I discovered four steps that were present in almost everything I read, so I'm including them in the following exercise.

1. Ask the person whose aura you want to see to stand or sit in front of a white background.
2. Choose a spot on the person and focus your attention on that spot for at least 30 seconds to a minute.

3. While continuing to focus on the chosen spot, allow yourself to look around the person's body with your peripheral vision.

4. It's important to continue to concentrate on the focus area and allow your peripheral vision to show you the aura without looking away from the focus spot.

5. Don't worry if you don't see anything the first time. In time, you will—or you won't—not everyone does.

## Auric Layers

We're making great progress! We now know what the aura is and have an exercise to help us develop our aura-seeing skills. In order to begin interpreting what we see, let's examine some basic information about the auric layers, and what the different shades of colors indicate. Let's start with the auric layers. Here's **some basic information** about our twelve auric layers, which reside in the physical, astral, spiritual, cosmic, and universal planes:

The **PHYSICAL PLANE** contains the first 3 layers:

**Layer #1: Etheric Body**

The 1st layer is related to the first/root chakra and bridges the connection of the material body to the higher bodies. It's about an inch or so out and around our body, and while invisible to most, some see it as a grayish-whitish outline around the body.

**Layer #2: Emotional Body**

The 2nd layer is associated with our second/sacral chakra. It's about three inches out and around our body, and our feelings are linked to this layer.

**Layer #3: Mental body**

The 3rd layer is associated with the ego and our third/solar plexus chakra. It extends approximately 3-8 inches out and around our body.

The **ASTRAL PLANE** contains the 4th layer:

**Layer #4: Astral Body**

The 4th layer is associated with our fourth/heart chakra and the way we express ourselves physically, emotionally, and mentally. It extends approximately 6-12 inches out and around our body.

The **SPIRITUAL PLANE** contains layers 5-7:

**Layer #5: Etheric Body**

The 5th layer is associated with our fifth/throat chakra. This layer affects our physical body and extends approximately 18-24 inches out and around our body. According to Dr. Pamela Nine (www.pamelanine.com), this is the layer where sound creates matter.

**Layer #6: Celestial Body**

The 6th layer is associated with processes of enlightenment and our sixth/brow or third eye chakra. It's located approximately 2-3 feet out and around our body.

**Layer #7: Causal Body**

The 7th layer is associated with our seventh/crown chakra and contains the life plan for our current incarnation. This layer extends 2-3 ½ feet out and around our body.

The **COSMIC PLANE** contains layers 8-10:

**Layer # 8: Memory Body**

The 8th layer of our aura is called the "memory body" and is associated with our eighth chakra. It connects us to the Akashic Records and karmic memories. Look for this layer extending upward approximately 1-3 feet above our body.

**Layer #9: Soul Body**

The 9th layer is also called the "soul level" and is related to our ninth chakra. It is connected to Divine Order and contracts and is located a few inches above our head.

**Layer #10: Integrative Body**

The tenth layer serves as a pathway between the physical and spiritual worlds and is associated with our tenth chakra. You will find this auric layer between the physical body and the etheric body.

The **UNIVERSAL PLANE** contains layers 11 & 12:

**Layer #11: Eternal Body**

This auric layer is the eternal body or eternal soul level and is associated with ascension. It is related to the eleventh chakra and is connected to and above the memory body (Layer 8) in a mushroom type shape.

**Layer: #12: Universal Mind Body**

This layer is said to be connected to Universal Consciousness, Ascended Masters and the Source and is related to the twelfth chakra. It penetrates the other auric layers.

There's much more to our auras than the little bit I've included above. If you're interested in studying them further, there are many wonderful books available. I also recommend taking a look at Dr. Pamela Nine's website (www.pamelanine.com). She's an internationally known intuitive counselor and spiritual medium. When I was researching information about the auric layers, I found her site to be detailed, well-organized, and easy to understand. And if you do decide to study auras further, here's a website titled Reiki for Holistic Health that includes a comprehensive list of the meanings of auric colors: www.reiki-for-holistic-health.com/auracolormeanings.html.

# Chapter Seventeen: Our Chakras

Here are our goals for this chapter:

1. to acquire an understanding of why it's so important to balance our chakras, and
2. to learn how our chakras work within our bodies.

Even though many say that there are up to 4,000 chakras in and around our bodies, we're going to focus on the seven main chakras because balancing them is job #1 for attaining health, happiness, and raising our vibrations in the *here and now*.

**What Are Chakras?**

Chakras are energy centers that are located both inside and outside of our bodies, and within our aura. They are often described as spinning vortexes or wheels of energy that run throughout our bodies and along our spines. In fact, "chakra" is the Sanskrit word for "circular motion," and the word "chakra" is very often translated as "wheel." If you visualize a wheel spinning in a circular motion, you'll have a good idea of what a chakra looks like. When they're functioning properly, they appear to be whirring *and* moving in a circular motion in the same clockwise direction.

Not only do we have chakras along our spine; we also have them above and below our bodies. For the most part, chakras are invisible to the human eye, but sometimes energy workers, like those who are trained in Reiki, and others (like you and me) can see them. We don't need special training to see auras and chakras. We just need to be open to seeing them, able to focus and concentrate, and be aware. Most people who *can* see them, say that individually our chakras look like balls of energy while others say that they have petal-like openings. Again, we don't need to see chakras to balance them. Balancing them, not seeing them, is what will keep us healthier and happier and raise our vibrations.

## Location of the Seven Main Chakras

With the exception of the first and seventh chakra, our chakras are aligned in sequence along our spine, neck, and skull. The illustration that follows was found on Wikipedia: Wikipedia/wiki/Chakra.

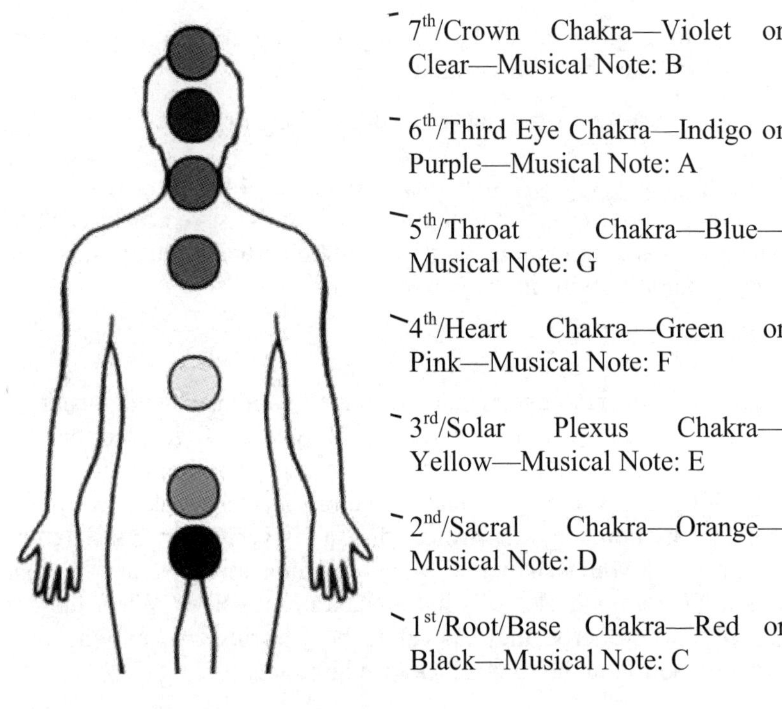


## Brief Information on the Chakras

**1st Chakra**: There is no nice way to describe where the first chakra, also called the **root or base chakra**, is located. It's positioned at our perineum, which is situated between the sexual organs and the anus. Some even say it extends a little bit out of our body. The energy the root chakra supplies creates the will to live and is involved with our need for food, shelter, clothing, and the basic necessities of life.

**2nd Chakra**: The second chakra, also called the **sacral chakra**, is located just above the pubic bone. It supplies energy for sexuality, reproduction, the enjoyment of life, and the physical attraction in relationships. It is also one of the areas where guilt is hidden.

**3rd Chakra**: The third chakra, also known as the **solar plexus chakra**, is located just below the sternum near the diaphragm. This chakra is involved with self-expression, taking action in the world, confidence, and personal power. It can also be a place where fear and anger are held. This is your "gut instinct."

**4th Chakra**: Our fourth chakra is called our **heart chakra**, and it's right in the center of our chest. This chakra supplies energy for all aspects of love, joy, compassion, and surrender. It supplies all parts of the energy field with nurturing and can be a source of spiritual connection and guidance.

**5th Chakra**: Our fifth chakra is located in our throat and not surprisingly is also called the **throat chakra**. It supplies energy for speaking, thinking, communicating, writing, and creative expression. The throat chakra can also be involved with clairaudience, contemplation, and inner guidance. It is one pathway through which our feelings are expressed. Clairaudience means clear hearing.

**6th Chakra**: Our sixth chakra is in the center of our forehead between the eyes, and it's also called the **brow** or the **third-eye chakra**. It supplies energy for self-awareness, inner vision, higher consciousness, clairvoyance, conceptual thinking, planning, and insight. In meditation, the third eye is a pathway to higher dimensions and higher consciousness. Clairvoyance means clear seeing.

**7th Chakra**: Our seventh chakra is right on top of our heads and points upward. It's also called the **crown chakra**. The crown chakra's energy connects with the spiritual realms, including higher consciousness and the Higher Power. It is one of the pathways to enlightenment.

## Chakra Functions

We know what our chakras are and where the seven main chakras are located, so let's take a look at their primary functions and how they work. Our chakras have two primary functions:

1. to vitalize or bolster the physical body in order to keep our bodies healthy and strong; and
2. to bring about the development of our consciousness so that we are strong both mentally and spiritually.

Basically, our seven major chakras deal with and help regulate our emotions, our spirituality, and our health, and they accomplish this because each one of our chakras is attached to or responsible for different body systems and organs. As such, each chakra corresponds to different areas of our bodies and different aspects of our psyche, which is why physical and psychological problems show up in a person's auric/energy field and chakras *long before* physical symptoms begin to appear in the physical body. It's all about our energy flow. When our *energy flow* is disrupted—that is, if we experience physical or emotional events that affect our energy centers—our chakras can become unbalanced or blocked."

**Effects of Disrupted Energy Flow & Blocked Chakras**

The normal struggles and occurrences of everyday life can and do affect the flow of energy through our chakras, and most of us deal with stressful situations every day of our lives. Here are some of the things we, as human beings, deal with that cause energy blockages—and there are times when we find ourselves dealing with more than one of them at a time:

- emotional upsets
- conflicts
- loss
- being involved in an accident
- stressful environment
- fear
- anxiety

Truly, anything that's outside our normal routine could negatively affect our energy flow, and so it follows that feeling depressed, unhappy, and even angry are **symptoms** of blocked energy and malfunctioning chakras. These *symptoms* are our body's way of saying, "Something's out of whack! It's time to balance me!"

Once we have this basic understanding that when our energy flow is constricted, it affects our physical, emotional, mental and/or spiritual bodies, it becomes much easier for us to go to the next level, which is grasping the concept that unbalanced chakras can lead to feelings of stress, unhappiness, depression, *and* physical illness.

Logically speaking then, taking the time to understand how our chakras work and learning the simple steps necessary to keep them in balance is how we as human beings can be proactive when it comes to our health and happiness *and* begin to vibrate at the highest level possible. Wouldn't you agree?

Good! Because taking the time to understand our chakras and keeping them in balance absolutely puts us firmly in control of our own health and happiness, and this is a very big deal—recognizing that we have this power.

**Benefits of Balanced Chakras**

When our seven major chakras are balanced and our life energy is flowing freely through them, we enjoy four main benefits:

1. Our bodies and minds are in balance, and we have a sense of physical, emotional, mental, and spiritual well-being.
2. Our bodies and minds are communicating with each other, and we are happier and healthier. This is because when the physical body is in a state of well-being, the mind, body, and spirit are at ease.
3. When our chakras are balanced and our energy is flowing freely, a state of mental clarity is attained and our emotions are peaceful—the world feels right and things are good.
4. Also, our energetic vibrational rate rises. The higher our vibrational level, the more we get out of our meditation sessions. The more we get out of our meditation sessions, the more open we are to experiencing our true Divine nature and our connection with Spirit and the Source/Creator/God. In fact, when all of our chakras are vibrating at their correct frequency *at the same time*, our physical, emotional, mental, and spiritual vibrations are increased.

That's a lot of benefits to be had just by taking a few minutes once or twice a week to keep our chakras tuned and balanced!

**Prana, Chi, & Ganglias**

I know. I know. You want to know how to balance your chakras, and we're getting to that, I promise. I don't want you to merely balance your chakras though. I want you to understand how they work; and I especially want you to understand that balancing our chakras isn't some New Age mumbo jumbo—*it's ancient wisdom.*

If you've read my other books, you know that I'm a big believer in yoga as a way to balance our minds and bodies. For centuries yogis have taught that chakras are centers of spiritual energy, and that this energy is called "prana" or "life force" energy. When we practice yoga, our blockages become unblocked, and our life force energy or prana flows freely. Let's talk a little chakra history.

- From the Hindu tradition of Yoga and the Yogis, we learn that each chakra contains a definitive number of *nadis* (pronounced Naydees) and that these nadis possess a tone or vibration.
- *Nadis are channels for the flow of consciousness*, and they work the same way that direct current (DC) moves negative and positive electrons through an electrical circuit.
- According to the tantras (ancient Hindu scriptures), there are 72,000 nadis channels or networks in our bodies through which our prana/life force/spiritual energy flows from one point to another.

The chakra centers circulate the pranic energy, and that energy is activated at and through the chakra centers. So in a way, our chakras are like individual power plants strategically located inside our bodies, sending energy to the particular parts of the physical, emotional, and mental bodies to which they correspond. In yoga, the union of prana and mind with self is the goal, and balancing our chakras helps that union of body, mind, and spirit happen.

The term *prana* to describe our energy flow is of Indian/Hindu origin, and as we reach out and study different traditions, it's remarkable to see that ancient wisdom about our energy flow is shared among many cultures and simply called by different names. For example, there's another term for *prana* that's of Chinese origin, and I'm sure you're familiar with this term: *chi*. The concept of chi is a perfect example of this shared wisdom. The similarities between prana and chi are startling. Let's take a look at ancient Chinese tradition for a moment:

- The Chinese call our life force energy "chi."
- The energy of chi emits color, vibrational frequency, and sound;
- When chi becomes disturbed, stagnant, imbalanced or depleted, dis-ease and illness begin to take form. When this happens, the aura becomes darker and discolored, personal frequency vibrates incorrectly, and the meridians become blocked.
- Meridians are what the Chinese call the "energy pathways" throughout the body, and we already know that the *Hindu* tradition refers to them as nadis.

These two philosophies are almost identical, and when we see this information coming up over and over again in the history of so many different cultures, we know on a soul level that it's something important that we need to pay attention to. Whether we call our life force "prana" or "chi," or whether we say that our life force flows through nadis or meridians doesn't matter. What *matters* is that we recognize that we *have* a life force, and by keeping our bodies in balance, we will live happier, healthier lives and enjoy a higher vibrational level.

A little more anatomy and I promise we'll get to the chakra balancing. Just as there are seven main chakras, we have seven main nerve ganglia in our bodies. Wait until you see where they're located. *Our seven main chakras inhabit the same space as our seven main nerve ganglia!* In fact, just look at this:

- The first five chakras (the root through the throat) correspond with the five main nerve ganglia of the spinal column—this is where our nerve endings form junctions. It's at these nerve ganglia where nerves from different organs and parts of the body join the spinal cord.
- The other two nerve ganglia are the upper and lower areas of the brain, and they correspond with the third eye and crown chakras.
- Our nerves sprout off from our nerve ganglia into our organs, body parts, and spinal cord.

Modern science tells us that if something upsets our nerve ganglia, our organs are affected. *Could it be* that that our organs are affected because the flow of chi or life energy has been slowed or stalled? If our ganglia were out of whack, would an allopathic doctor want to get them back on track? The answer to both of these questions is a resounding, "Yes!" And since our chakras inhabit the same space as our nerve ganglia; rational and logical thinking dictates that keeping our chakras balanced will have a positive effect on our health and well-being.

To get the full picture, visualize your chakras as pumps or valves that regulate the flow of energy throughout the entire energy system of our bodies. If our energy system is "out of whack," so are we for these reasons:

- Every time we make a decision or choice about how we're going to act, react, think or feel about something, our chakra valves open and close accordingly.
- The balanced or unbalanced functioning of our chakras reflects the decisions we make with regard to how we choose to respond to what's going on in our lives, and this affects our health and well-being.

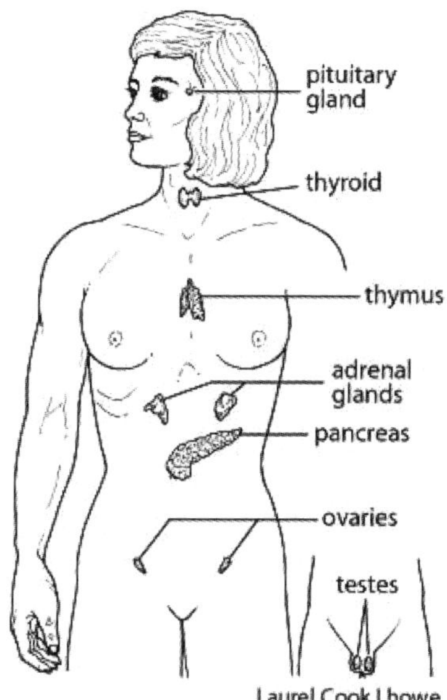


Let's take this a step further. *Our chakra valves* interact with our physical bodies through two major vehicles: **the endocrine system and the nervous system.** The picture of the glands of the endocrine system was found at this website:http://science.yourdictionary.com/endocrine-systemseven.html.

Each one of our seven main chakras is associated with one of the seven endocrine glands, as well as with a group of nerves called a plexus.

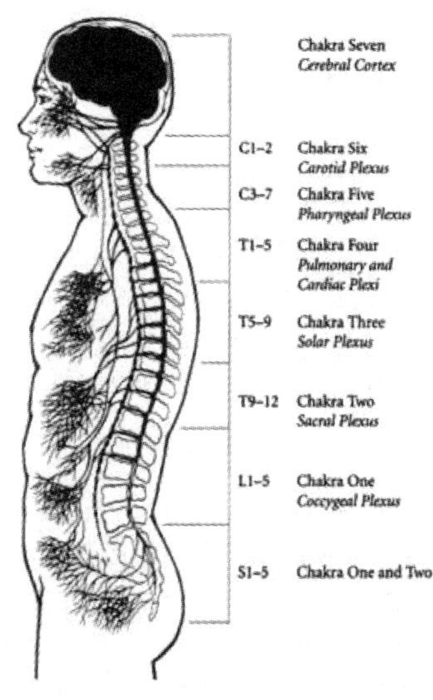


See ww.realmagick.com/nerve-ganglia for the drawing.

When we are tense, it's detected in our chakra by the nerves of the plexus associated with that chakra, and then that tension is transmitted to the parts of the body controlled by that plexus. Thus it is that we are one big electrical system! When this kind of tension continues over a period of time or is of a high level of intensity, symptoms are then created on a physical level. *What disturbs our minds will also disturb our bodies*.

Quick reminder: symptoms are not the dis-ease. Symptoms are our body's way of communicating to us that something is wrong. Fix the underlying problem that's causing the symptoms, and the symptoms go away. In this way, we can view the chakras as a kind of roadmap to our health and happiness.

Great job absorbing the anatomy lesson! Now let's look at the different ways we can balance our chakras.

## Chakra Balancing Using Yoga

I can't say enough about the mental and physical benefits of a yoga practice. Practicing yoga helps us keep our chakras well-oiled, balanced, and vibrant. We can practice yoga alone, or we can do it in groups, at home, or at a studio. If you are a newcomer to yoga, I suggest that you take several yoga classes with a trained yoga instructor to learn how to do the poses/asanas correctly. Once we learn how to properly do the poses, yoga is a flexible and convenient way to keep our chakras in tip top condition and to keep our prana flowing, too, as yoga balances our mind and body and helps us open up to Spirit.

## Chakra Balancing Using Reiki

Another way to get our energy flowing properly and balance our chakras is with Reiki (pronounced Ray-Key). Reiki is of Japanese origin, which is yet another ancient culture that advocates the proper flow of energy in our bodies to promote health and happiness. Reiki is a technique for stress reduction and relaxation that also promotes healing. It's administered by *the laying on of hands* and based on the idea that an *unseen life force energy or ki (think prana or chi)* flows through us.

Reiki practitioners say that if one's life force energy is low, then we're more likely to get sick or feel stress; and if it is high, we're more capable of being happy and healthy. The word *Reiki* is made up of two Japanese words: *Rei*, which means "God's Wisdom or the Higher Power" and *Ki*, which means "life force energy;" therefore, the practice of Reiki is actually "spiritually guided life force energy."

Reiki Masters, as well as other energy workers, balance our chakras by channeling healing energy through touch points in the body (think nadis or meridians). They clear our energy field of blockages, so that our chakras are balanced and spinning freely and properly.

Like yoga, we can take classes and learn Reiki or other energy healing modalities so we can do this for ourselves, but it just makes sense to work with a professional when we're first starting out to make sure that we're doing everything properly.

## Chakra Balancing Using Color

Here's a quick review of what our seven major chakras are called, and the colors associated with them:

| | | |
|---|---|---|
| **1st chakra** | Root or Base | Red or Black |
| **2nd chakra** | Sacral | Orange |
| **3rd chakra** | Solar Plexus | Yellow |
| **4th chakra** | Heart | Green or Pink |
| **5th chakra** | Throat | Sky Blue |
| **6th chakra** | Third Eye or Brow | Indigo Blue or Purple |
| **7th chakra** | Crown | Clear or Violet |

Incorporating color into our basic meditation routine or developing a color-based meditation are both excellent ways to keep our chakras balanced and our chi flowing. Here's why:

- All colors are individual frequencies of energy, and each of our chakras vibrates at a specific color frequency, which means that our chakras are energy vortexes vibrating at specific levels of color.
- By visualizing the colors associated with each chakra, we can balance them.
- By understanding how individual colors affect and influence us, we can learn to spot symptoms of dis-ease and work with color to balance our chakras as needed.

There's actually a lot of evidence supporting the fact that color influences people and has a physical effect on the human body.

Scientifically speaking, colors influence the pituitary gland, which helps regulate hormone production. We all know that hormones affect our moods, so it's not really a big jump to say that color affects our moods. After all, how many times have you heard or said the following:

- "He was green with envy."
- "He saw red."
- "She's feeling blue today."

It's almost as if we have an innate understanding of the significance of color; and no one understands the significance and effect that color has on us better than advertising companies. They help their clients choose the colors of their sign, packaging, and advertising pieces based on color *because* color affects us mentally and physically. McDonald's is a textbook example of a company that uses color to influence potential customers. They use lots of red and yellow—and here's why: red stimulates the appetite, so we buy more, and yellow is attention getting—the perfect color to pull us into those golden arches. Red and yellow are the perfect combination of colors to manipulate us mentally and physically to hungrily enter their stores and upsize our order. And McDonald's isn't alone. Take a drive down the main street in your town and look at the restaurant signs. You'll see lots of red and yellow, and blue, too. Why blue? What's the color of uniforms for most police, security guards, and airlines? Blue indicates dependability.

You get the idea. Color affects us, so how do we use color to balance our chakras? It's easy. Try one of these ways:

- Simply picture each chakra by color and visualize it vibrating and whirring and spinning in a clockwise direction.
- To add color to my meditation, I hold a stone or crystal that's the color of the chakra I want to balance.
- You can also combine visualizing the color of the specific chakra and holding the crystal.

- If you're working with stones and crystals, you can lie down for your meditation and lay them on your chakra points.

**Shelly Wilson's Quick Chakra Balancing Exercise Using Color**

Here's a quick chakra balancing exercise utilizing color that Author, Reiki Master/Intuitive Medium Shelly Wilson incorporates into her workshops. She very kindly is allowing me to include it here so we can clear our energetic clutter and revitalize our energy. This meditation is on the CD accompanying this book, and you will find another chakra balancing exercise at the end of this section.

**Take a moment to just BE**. Sit in a chair with your back straight and your palms up (open to receiving). Close your eyes. You may want to visualize the chakras and their respective colors as fruits, vegetables, or even flowers.

- **Begin with the root chakra**. This is your area of survival needs and where the lower energies of fear, doubt, worry, anger, and frustration reside. Visualize it as red, beautiful, healthy, balanced and cleared.

Deeply breathe in green healing energy from Archangel Raphael and exhale anything and anyone that no longer serves you.

- **Move up to the sacral chakra.** This is your area of creativity. Visualize it as orange: beautiful, healthy, balanced and cleared.

Deeply breathe in green healing energy from Archangel Raphael and exhale anything and anyone that no longer serves you.

- **Move up to the solar plexus chakra**. This is your gut instinct. Visualize it as yellow: beautiful, healthy, balanced and cleared.

Deeply breathe in green healing energy from Archangel Raphael and exhale anything and anyone that no longer serves you.

- **Move up to the heart chakra**. Allow your chest to expand and your heart to open fully to receive the love that is all around you. Visualize it as green: beautiful, healthy, balanced and cleared.

Deeply breathe in green healing energy from Archangel Raphael. Allow this energy to fill your lungs and your heart and flow through your veins. Exhale anything and anyone that no longer serves you.

- **Move up to the throat chakra**. This is your voice and your area of communication. Allow yourself to communicate your needs and desires to yourself and others. Visualize it as sky blue: beautiful, healthy, balanced and cleared.

Deeply breathe in green healing energy from Archangel Raphael and exhale anything and anyone that no longer serves you and prevents you from speaking your truth.

- **Move up to the third eye.** This is your area of psychic awareness. Visualize it as indigo: beautiful, healthy, balanced and cleared.

Deeply breathe in green healing energy from Archangel Raphael and exhale anything and anyone that no longer serves you.

- **Lastly, you are at the crown chakra**, your connection to Source, The Higher Power, All That Is. Visualize it as pure white light, beautiful, healthy, balanced and clear.

Deeply breathe in green healing energy from Archangel Raphael and exhale anything and anyone that no longer serves you. Once again, breathe in deeply the healing energy; and exhale your pain, worry, fear, frustration, anger, and anything and everything that no longer serves you. Release and let it go!

Your chakras have been cleared and balanced. You are love and you are loved. And so it is!

Thank you, Shelly! At the end of this chapter, you'll find individual sections with information about each of the seven major chakras, and these sections include the in-depth meanings of the colors associated with each chakra. These sections also list crystals and stones that work well with each chakra.

## Chakra Balancing Using Sound

Let's look at the following chart to see the musical notes that are associated with each chakra.

| | | | |
|---|---|---|---|
| **1st chakra** | Root/Base | Red or Black | C |
| **2nd chakra** | Sacral | Orange | D |
| **3rd chakra** | Solar Plexus | Yellow | E |
| **4h chakra** | Heart | Green or Pink | F |
| **5th chakra** | Throat | Sky Blue | G |
| **6th chakra** | Third Eye | Indigo Blue or Purple | A |
| **7th chakra** | Crown | Violet or Clear | B |

Our chakras vibrate, and *the most elemental state of vibration is sound.* Therefore, it stands to reason that *everything* has an *optimal range of vibration.* Scientists call that optimum range of vibration "resonance." When we are in resonance, we are in balance.

Every organ and every cell in our body absorbs and emits sound, *and so* every organ has its own optimum resonance frequency.

Colors are sounds, resonating at a higher frequency; *therefore,* we can use *color* and *sound* to bring our body *into resonance.*

According to Ancient Hindu beliefs, everything in the universe is made of sound, and each chakra has what is called a "seed sound." These seed sounds (more about them shortly) are the symbolic representations of the energy pattern of each chakra and hold its essence. What this means for us is that we can directly influence the resonance/the balance of our bodies by using sound to balance our chakras. And, conveniently for us, each chakra is associated with a specific musical note.

Anyone who plays an instrument started out by learning this beginning scale: C, D, E, F, G, A, B. From the root to the crown, memorize this scale and you'll remember the notes that will balance each of your seven main chakras. To add sound to your meditation, try one of these suggestions:

- During meditation, say or chant the mantra/seed sound (see **Chakra Balancing: Seed Sounds** as follows) for each chakra as you picture it.
- Sing, hum, or use an instrument to produce the notes associated with each chakra. Visualize each chakra as you sing, hum, or strike the note. Follow the scale above.

Many people also use crystal bowls and tuning forks to help them resonate with and balance their chakras. Also, there are lots of great chakra balancing CDs that incorporate the correct notes and seed sounds that you can buy and listen to while you meditate.

**Chakra Balancing Using Seed Sounds/Mantras**

Let's talk a little bit more about seed sounds. Everything in the universe is made of sound, and each chakra has its own *seed sound.* A seed sound is the symbolic representation of the energy pattern of each chakra and holds its essence. Seed sounds are also referred to as *mantras*, such as Ohm, pronounced "*aaAAuuuMMMmmm*," which we're all familiar with. When properly spoken, the person performing the mantra resonates with the associated chakra.

Adding seed sounds/mantras is an easy way to add sound to your chakra meditation. It does take a little practice at first, but it's a powerful form of meditation because the sound helps open our chakra points more quickly. You'll have the sounds down in no time, and because we're using our voices, mantras are always available as a chakra balancing tool.

If you choose to work with them, the mantras or seed sounds can be chanted individually if you are working on one particular area, or you can chant them one after the other to balance your entire chakra system.

Here's a list of the seed sounds and mantras for each chakra; the CD accompanying this book has the correct pronunciation of each seed sound so you can practice:

**Base/1st Chakra/Red • LAM • "C"**

Curve the tip of your tongue up and back, and place it on the rear section of the upper palate to pronounce a sound like the word ***alum*** without the initial *a*.

{LuuuUUUMMMMmmm}

**Sacral/2nd Chakra/Orange • VAM • "D"**

Place the upper set of teeth on the inner section of your lower lip and begin with a breathy consonant to imitate the sound of a fast car. Pronounce the mantra like ***fvam.***

{FvaaaAAAMMMMMmmm}

**Solar Plexus/3rd Chakra/Yellow • RAM • "E"**

Place the tip of your tongue on the roof of the front section of the upper palate, roll the r like in Spanish and pronounce the mantra like the first part of the word ***rum****-ble*.

{RuuUUMMMMMMmmm}

**Heart/4th Chakra/Green • HAM • "F"**

Pronounce it by inhaling audibly through your mouth and pronounce the word ***hum*** (as in humming); allow the breath to extend beyond the resolution of the consonant.

{HuUUMMMMMMMmmm}

**Throat/5th Chakra/Blue • YAM • "G"**

Pronounce it by inhaling noiselessly through your mouth and pronounce the sound like the word ***yum*** (as in yummy); allow the sound along with your breath to fill your mouth and throat cavity.

{YuUUMMMMMMMmmm}

**Third Eye/6th Chakra/Indigo/Purple • SHAM • "A"**

Pronounced *shum*, this sound is formed in the later part of the palate.

{ShuuMMMMMMmmm}

**Crown/7th Chakra/Violet/Clear • OM • "B"**

Om is pronounced ***aum*** by inhaling audibly through your nostrils and directing the stream of air to the point between your eyebrows. Pronounce the sound along with your exhalation as a subtly audible whisper, allowing the sound and breathe to resonate in the cranial area.

{aaaAAUUMMMMMMMmmm}

**Chakra Balancing Meditation with Color and Seed Sounds**

This meditation incorporates both color and sound. You can memorize it, or you can play the CD that accompanies this book, and I'll guide you through it.

**Preparation for Meditation**

- Sit up straight, spine erect with both feet on the ground.
- Let your arms rest comfortably by your sides or on your lap.
- Take a deep breath in through your nose, and then breathe out through your nose. Take another deep breath in through your nose, and then out through your nose.
- Take a few more deep breaths, and as you're breathing, feel your breathing becoming deeper—nice even, deep breaths in and out.
- Continue breathing and visualize yourself standing with your feet apart, hands by your sides, and with your fingers naturally open.
- Keep this picture in your mind as you continue to inhale and exhale. Allow your breathing to relax your body and clear your mind.

**Meditation**

- Now, visualize a **red** circle of energy near the **base of your spine**. This is your base chakra and the energy is strong. It connects you to the Earth and generates instinctive feelings of survival. It urges you to love and care for yourself. Feel and see this red wheel vibrating and spinning as you relax into its beautiful energy and chant the seed sound to open and balance this chakra: **LuuuUUUMMMMmmm. (Repeat 3 times.)**
- Now that your root chakra is balanced, move your attention upward to the next circle of energy, an **orange** wheel of energy **in your pelvic area**. This is your s**acral chakra**, the center of your emotions.

Your acceptance of pleasure springs from this energy source. Visualize yourself accepting the joy and contentment that contributes to the overall balance of your life. Stay here for a few moments and bask in the orange light as you balance your sacral chakra. It begins to whirr with vibrant orange vibrational energy as you chant the seed sound to open and balance this chakra: **FvaaaAAAMMMMMmmm. (Repeat 3 times.)**

- Check your breathing: Breathe in deeply and exhale deeply as you prepare to move further up your spine to your s**olar plexus chakra**. Move your attention now to the **bright yellow** circle of energy **near your navel**.

Your personal power flows from this chakra; the essence of your spirituality begins with this positive energy source, vibrating and spinning now with your root and sacral chakras, as you chant the seed sound **RuuUUMMMMMMmmm** to open and balance this chakra. **(Repeat 3 times.)**

- Move your attention now up to your **heart chakra** in the **center of your chest**. Your heart chakra is a **green** ball of energy, and its vibration is about love.

It is the source of active love that is in everything you do. Your ability to love comes from here and includes your capacity for empathy, sympathy, forgiveness, and allows the abundance of all life to be available to you.

The positive essence of this chakra is an overwhelming sense of fullness felt as love. Visualize now your vibrant green heart chakra whirring and spinning as you balance its energy by chanting its seed sound to bring it into sync with the first three chakras: **HuUUMMMMMMMmmm. (Repeat 3 times.)**

- And now, slowly move your attention further up your body to your t**hroat chakra**, which holds the **blue** energy of your own inner voice. Feel it guiding you to be open and honest with yourself and with others. This is your voice of wisdom. When listened to, this blue energy will lead you to take actions that will keep you balanced and true to yourself.

Visualize now a bright blue ball or wheel, the color of the blue sky, whirring and spinning as you balance this vibration within your body with its seed sound: **YuUUMMMMMMMmmm. (Repeat 3 times.)**

- Move your attention slowly now to the next chakra point, your t**hird eye chakra**. This **deep indigo** energy center is in your **brow area between your eyebrows**. Your third eye will guide you to awareness of your soul. Imagination is the magic of this chakra.

Let yourself free your mind. As you accept the power and the awe of your own soul, you will recognize the soul within everyone and everything around you. Breathe deeply and chant the seed sound for your third eye chakra: **ShuuMMMMMMmmm. (Repeat 3 times.)**

- And now move your attention to the **top of your head**, where the c**rown chakra** is located. It is here the **brilliant violet** energy flows out and above you. This energy is directly connected to your spiritual self and all spirituality in the world. Once this chakra is balanced and aligned, flashes of enlightenment will occur—moments of true understanding of the world and all it contains.

All events and emotions become clear, and during those moments, everything makes sense. This Highest Energy Source is the essence of all life and existence. It is true magic and it is yours.

Watch it now as it vibrates and whirrs and aligns itself with the red, orange, yellow, green, blue, and indigo wheels of energy as you complete the balancing of your chakras with the seed sound for your crown chakra: **aaaAAOOOOUUMMMMMmmm. (Repeat 3 times.)**

- Visualize now **all seven chakras**—red, orange, yellow, green, blue, indigo, and violet—vibrating in perfect alignment with one another as they spin brilliantly in a clockwise direction. And take a few minutes to enjoy the energy flowing throughout your entire being.

Feel the sensations of peace and happiness as your body and mind connect and communicate and enjoy this newly balanced energy.

Know the feeling of being fully energized and balanced.

**Closing the Meditation**

- And now, as you begin to bring yourself back into a state of wakefulness, know that these feelings of peace, joy, and happiness are the natural state for a human being, and you deserve to feel this way every day.
- And as you begin to ground yourself, move your hands and fingers, your toes and feet. Roll your head in a circle and when you are ready, open your eyes and take your joy and happiness out into the world and share it with your family, friends, co-workers, and everyone you meet.

Namaste.

Next is an in-depth look at each of our seven major chakras, including the meanings of the colors associated with them and which crystals and stones work well when it comes to balancing them.

**The Root/Base Chakra (First Chakra)**

The root/base chakra is related to survival, our body and identity as an individual. Our health, constitution and security, including material wealth are also linked to the root chakra. The energy the root chakra supplies creates the will to live and is involved with our need for food, shelter, clothing, and the basic necessities of life. The root/base chakra is about being physically here and at home in situations.

**If it is open**, you feel grounded, stable and secure. You will be present in the *here and now* and connected to your physical body. In addition, you will feel good both physically and emotionally about yourself when you look in the mirror.

**If your root chakra is weak, closed, or underactive**, you may have feelings of unworthiness, nervousness, fearfulness, and/or and not be comfortable in your own skin.

**If this chakra is overactive**, you may be materialistic and greedy. You may be obsessed with being secure and resist change.

| **Sanskrit Name** | Muladhara chakra |
|---|---|
| **Color** | Red |
| **Musical Note** | C |
| **Mantra and Seed Sound** | LAM (Pronounced "Lum")<br>(LuuUUUUMmmmm) |
| **Location** | Perineum (point between the sexual organs & anus) |
| **Parts of the Body** | Large intestine, rectum, hips, thighs |
| **Endocrine Gland** | Adrenal glands (produces the hormones cortisol, aldosterone, DHEA, adrenaline, non-adrenaline) |
| **Crystals/Stones** | Red jasper, ruby, garnet, red jade, red carnelian |

## Significance of the Color Red

Red is thought to connect us to our physical self and is thought to be associated with courage, strength, vitality, vigor, ambition, alertness, sexuality, a pioneering spirit, willpower, passion, aggressiveness, anger, fire, heat, embarrassment, life and lifeblood. Red is energizing and exciting, and here are some of the benefits of this color:

- overcoming negative thoughts, a sense of power and self-confidence;
- a feeling of security and safety;
- an appetite stimulant;
- chronic pain and migraine relief;
- stimulation of the automatic nervous and circulatory systems and the liver;
- help with female disorders;
- reduction of inflammation and swelling;
- strengthening the heart;
- building the blood;
- drawing poisons to a head to be eliminated; acts as a pustulant.

## The Sacral/Sexual Chakra (Second Chakra)

The sacral chakra, also called the sexual chakra, is located in the lower abdomen. This chakra is associated with emotions, feelings, states of desire and imagination. This chakra supplies energy for sexuality, reproduction, the enjoyment of life, and the physical attraction in relationships. It is also one of the areas where guilt is hidden.

**If your sacral chakra is open**, your feelings flow freely and are expressed without being overly emotional. You are open to intimacy and have no problems dealing with your sexuality. You are able to attract the right partners and enjoy compatible people who nourish you, fill you with joy, and make you a better person. You are also more self-confident and patient.

**If your sacral chakra is weak, closed, or underactive**, you tend to be stiff and unemotional or have a "poker face." Your partners are often wrong and incompatible for you, and you may find yourself wondering if you'll ever find "the one."

**If this chakra is overactive**, you may be overly emotional, frigid, anxious, frustrated, or over-sexed.

| | |
|---|---|
| **Sanskrit Name** | Swadisthana chakra |
| **Color** | Orange |
| **Musical Note** | D |
| **Mantra and Seed Sound** | VAM (Pronounced "Fvam") (FffVVAAAAAMMMMmmm) |
| **Location** | Abdomen center—midway between pubic bone and navel |
| **Parts of the Body** | Reproductive system--women's sexual organs, kidneys, bladder |
| **Endocrine Gland** | Ovaries |
| **Crystals/Stones** | Orange carnelian, amber, golden topaz, citrine, orange calcite |

**Significance of the Color Orange**

Orange is thought to connect us to our emotional self and is associated with sociability, social confidence, success, happiness, and resourcefulness. It's said to relieve worry and anxiety and is stimulating—but not as much as the color red. More benefits of the color orange are said to be these:

- an increase of optimism, personal power, self-esteem;
- helps expand interests and activities;
- helps people handle the ups and downs of life more easily;
- helps remove inhibitions;
- increases creativity, inspiration, and intuition;
- helps with stiff lower back, bladder, bowel and lower intestines, all bladder, kidney problems;
- relieves rheumatism, arthritis, exhaustion, eating disorders, food allergies; and
- helps stabilize the pulse rate.

**The Solar Plexus Chakra (Third Chakra)**

The solar plexus chakra is located an inch or two above the navel. This chakra is the focal point for your power and will, ego and authority, as well as self-motivation and discipline. The solar plexus chakra is involved with taking action with confidence in the world. This is your "gut instinct." It is also about asserting yourself in a group.

**If your solar plexus chakra is open**, you feel in control and have sufficient self-esteem. You are confident, feel empowered, and desire others to feel the same.

**If your solar plexus chakra is weak, closed, or underactive,** you may tend to be passive, indecisive, unworthy, or guilty.

**If this chakra is overactive**, you may be domineering, aggressive, or angry.

| Sanskrit Name | Manipura chakra |
|---|---|
| Color | Yellow |
| Musical Note | E |
| Mantra and Seed Sound | RAM (Pronounced "Rum")<br>RuuMMMMMmmmm |
| Location | A couple inches above the navel |
| Parts of the Body | Stomach, liver, gall bladder, nervous system, spleen, pancreas, small intestine |
| Endocrine Gland | Adrenal gland, |
| Crystals/Stones | Yellow jade, golden tiger eye, citrine, yellow calcite, yellow fluorite |

**Significance of the Color Yellow**

Yellow is thought to connect us to our mental self and is thought to be associated with mental clarity (clear mindedness), cheerfulness, optimism, and intellectual maturity. It's said to stimulate the thinking process and raise our spirits. Other benefits of the color yellow include:

- promotes wisdom and inspiration;
- assists concentration and memory;
- stimulates curiosity and interest;
- eases depression;
- helps with empowerment, confidence, and courage;
- helps lower anxiety;

- promotes energy;
- aids in discernment and decision making;
- help with night blindness (filters out blue light);
- increases metabolic rate;
- stimulates and builds nerves; and
- helps with rheumatoid arthritis, neuritis, and similar conditions (because yellow may help eliminate calcium and lime deposits)

**The Heart Chakra (Fourth Chakra)**

The heart chakra is located at the center of the chest and is associated with love and understanding, limitless compassion, empathy and forgiveness. The heart chakra supplies energy for all aspects of love, joy, compassion, and surrender. It supplies all parts of the energy field with nurturing and can be a source of spiritual connection and guidance. The heart chakra is about love, kindness, affection and inner harmony.

**When it is open**, you are compassionate and friendly. You enjoy comfortable, loving, and empathic relationships and get along well with family and friends.

**When your heart chakra is weak, closed, or underactive**, you may be cold, distant, emotionally unstable, and have emotional problems in relationships with others. You might feel sorrow and loss but can't get over the past and may tend to sabotage relationships and struggle with commitment.

**If your heart chakra is overactive,** you may become lazy, allow yourself to be walked on or taken advantage of. You may be moody or depressed.

| | |
|---|---|
| **Sanskrit Name** | Anahata chakra |
| **Color** | Green and pink |
| **Musical Note** | F |
| **Mantra and Seed Sound** | YAM (Prounounced "Hum" huuUUMMMMMMmmm |
| **Location** | Center of chest |
| **Parts of the Body** | Heart, circulatory system, lungs, blood, vagus nerve |
| **Endocrine Gland** | Thymus (controls immune system) |
| **Crystals/Stones** | Green aventurine, pink and watermelon quartz, emerald, green agate, malachite, peridot<br>Rose quartz, pink agate, rhodochrosite, pink tourmaline |

**Significance of the Color Green**

Green is thought to connect us to unconditional love and be associated with peace, renewal, love, hope, balance, harmony, self-control, growth, and life. Green is revitalizing and calming; it's the color of nature and, therefore, associated with fertility and abundance. More benefits of the color green are thought to be to be as follows:

- stress reduction;
- calmness;
- rest and relaxation;
- sense of balance and normalcy;

- overall well-being;
- growth, abundance, prosperity, and hope;
- refreshing, peaceful, contentment; and
- luck, money, beauty.

**Significance of the Color Pink**

Both pink and green are often associated with the heart chakra, so let's look at the qualities of pink. You will see similar qualities of pink and green. Pink is thought to connect us to universal love and be associated with compassion and tolerance. More benefits of the color pink are thought to be as follows:

- emotional love of self and others;
- friendship, affection, and harmony;
- the ability to attract, increase, or strength love;
- self-confidence;
- the ability to smooth difficulties in relationships;
- inner peace and calmness.

**The Throat Chakra (Fifth Chakra)**

The throat chakra is located in the center of the throat near the Adam's apple. This chakra is linked to our ability to communicate. It supplies energy for speaking, communicating, writing, creativity and self-expression. The throat chakra is also associated with clairaudience, inspiration, peace, joy, and tranquility. It is one pathway through which our feelings are expressed.

**When the throat chakra is open**, you have no problems expressing yourself. You are tranquil, truthful, intuitive and trusting. You are good at voicing your thoughts, ideas and emotions to those around you and have good communication skills.

**When this chakra is weak, closed, or underactive**, you tend not to speak much and probably are introverted and shy. You may feel as if no one cares about your opinion and/or that you have nothing of value to say, but not speaking the truth may block this chakra.

**If this chakra is overactive**, you may talk too much, speak negatively or harshly, or gossip about others. You might also be domineering or over-react to people or situations. You might also be self-centered or self-righteous.

| **Sanskrit Name** | Visshuda chakra |
|---|---|
| **Color** | Blue |
| **Musical Note** | G |
| **Mantra and Seed Sound** | HAM (Pronounced "Yum") |
| **Location** | Throat |
| **Parts of the Body** | Throat, trachea, vocal cords, alimentary canal |
| **Endocrine Gland** | Thyroid (stores hormones that regulate the heart rate, blood pressure, body temperature, and the rate food is converted into energy |
| **Crystals/Stones** | Turquoise, blue lace agate, celestite, blue topaz, sodalite |

**Significance of the Color Blue**

Blue is thought to connect us to holistic thoughts-and is thought to be associated with communication, creativity, personal expression, vitality, decisiveness, knowledge, and health. It is the color of trustworthiness, and its soothing properties are thought to produce mental and spiritual tranquility. More benefits of the color blue are thought to be as follows:

- mental relaxation, calmness and peace;
- help with insomnia and sleep disorders;

- clear communication and calmness in speaking;
- help with hyperactivity in children;
- relaxes and calms muscles;
- relieves headaches and migraines;
- helps with fever, sore throats, laryngitis;
- improves listening skills;
- awakens intuition and eases loneliness.

**Third-Eye/Brow Chakra (Sixth Chakra)**

The third eye chakra is located in the center of the head between your eyebrows and up just a bit. This chakra is related to our ability to perceive clearly. Intuition, insight, and imagination are also associated with this chakra. The third eye chakra supplies energy for psychic abilities, clairvoyance, inner vision, perception, and projection.

**When the third eye chakra is open**, you have good intuition and use it to make good decisions. You are wise and intelligent and take action on your ideas. You see clearly and know where you are going in life.

**When it is weak, closed, or underactive**, you may have difficulty focusing in life, feel detached, experience intellectual fuzziness/ fogginess, and feel indecisive when faced with making decisions or judgment calls.

**If this chakra is overactive**, you may live too much in a world of fantasy and wishful thinking or feel like you are spiritually above others.

| **Sanskrit Name** | Ajna chakra |
|---|---|
| **Color** | Indigo, purple |
| **Musical Note** | A |
| **Mantra and Seed Sound** | SHAM (Pronounced “Shum”) (ShuuMMMMmmm) |
| **Location** | Between the eyebrows and a bit above |
| **Parts of the Body** | Lower brain, left eye, ears, nose, nervous system |
| **Endocrine Gland** | Pituitary (Master gland which acts as an intermediary between the brain and other endocrine glands) |
| **Crystals/Stones** | Iolite, blue topaz, blue jasper, indigo kyanite, lapis lazuli, fluorite, amethyst |

**Significance of the Color Indigo**

Indigo is thought to connect us to our spiritual self and is associated with inspiration, creativity, and beauty. The benefits of the color indigo are thought to include:

- concentration, imagination, focus, enhanced artistic ability;
- reduction of excitement and irritation;
- relaxes and calms nerves and lymphatic system;
- source of intuition, clairvoyance, and extrasensory perception;

- soothing effect on the eyes, ears, and nervous system;
- balancing influence that helps with fear, frustration, and any distortion of inner energies.

**Significance of the Color Purple**

Depending on what you read, you will find purple associated either with the third eye or the crown chakra. Purple is the color of spirituality and imagination. It urges us to find our power within—not the kind of power that needs to control or dominate others but power rooted in connection to Spirit. Purple is associated with wisdom, dignity, independence and creativity. It affects the pineal gland, top of the spinal cord, and the brain stem. It is an introspective color that lets us get in touch with our deeper thoughts.

Purple imparts determination and feelings of being in control, clears the mind of negative influences, calms nervousness and relieves stress. It symbolizes power, nobility, luxury, and sophistication. It is also said to have the ability to do the following:

- convey wealth and extravagance;
- symbolize magic and mystery;
- be useful in meditation to lead you deeper within;
- be uplifting;
- calm the mind and nerves; and
- encourage creativity and spirituality.

**The Crown Chakra (Seventh Chakra)**

The crown chakra is located at the very top of the head and points upward. This chakra is associated with divine wisdom, our Spirit, our oneness with the universe, our unity with all that is, and enlightenment. The crown chakra's energy connects us with the spiritual realms, including higher consciousness and the Higher Power. It is one of the pathways to enlightenment.

The crown chakra is about universal energy/cosmic consciousness, cosmic love, and spiritual awareness of the meaning of life.

**When this chakra is open**, you feel connected to a higher power, and will experience awareness of the meaning of life, cosmic consciousness, and enlightenment.

**If it is weak, closed, or underactive**, you're less aware of and close-minded about spirituality. With a $7^{th}$ chakra that is largely closed, you will feel separated from abundance and wholeness and won't be completely free of fear. This could lead to illness.

**If this chakra is overactive**, you could become ill as your body tries to tell you it's time to go within and learn the real meaning of life.

| | |
|---|---|
| **Sanskrit Name** | Sahasrara chakra |
| **Color** | Violet or Clear |
| **Musical Note** | B |
| **Mantra and Seed Sound** | Om<br>(aaaAAOOOUUMMMMMMmmm) |
| **Location** | Top of the head |
| **Parts of the Body** | Upper brain, right eye |
| **Endocrine Gland** | Pineal (regulates sleep cycle produces the hormone melatonin) |
| **Crystals/Stones** | Clear quartz, amethyst, diamond, lepidolite, lavender quartz, clear tourmaline, ametrine, iolite |

### Significance of the Color Violet

Violet, the color associated with the crown chakra, is of a very high frequency. This energy opens us to the gifts and possibilities that extend beyond our physical plane. It enhances our spiritual power and creativity and is sometimes called the color of the Spirit. It's been suggested that violet may help in these situations:

- when one is experiencing emotional challenges;
- when someone desires to strengthen creativity;
- when someone is seeking to strengthen spirituality;
- when trying to balance heaven and earth in your life;
- when one feels ready to open to Divine wisdom; and/or
- when one wishes to increase/speed up natural healing.

## Significance of the Color Clear

Clear crystals reflect all colors and are imbued with all of their energies. Clear quartz helps bring clarity to our communication and will amplify all the crystals it is used with. It is commonly used by healers as it has a positive effect on all the chakras since it protects the aura and expands the human energy field.

## 21st Century Chakra Wisdom

The study of the chakra system is a standard course of learning in the colleges of modern Eastern cultures, and understanding the chakra system is crucial in the universally accepted practices of acupuncture and acupressure. But what about Western medicine?

I'm very happy to report that even traditional Western doctors are getting onboard with this ancient wisdom. One example is Dr. Candace Pert, an internationally recognized pharmacologist with a degree from John Hopkins University of Medicine and tons of scientific credentials under her belt. She believes in chakras. Here's what she said in a *Washington Post* interview in February 2010:

*It's so fascinating how this ancient wisdom corresponds to modern science—I was shocked. My chakras were shocked! I realized in 1987 that areas along the axis from the top of the forehead to the base of the spine, these classical chakra areas, corresponded to what I called "nodal points"—places where lots of neurotransmitters and neuropeptides are released...I went to a meeting in '87 on AIDS Medicine and Miracles, and that's where someone showed me where the chakras are, and that's when I had the big "Aha!"—it literally blew my mind. You see, we scientists are very conservative and so this was almost frightening to see this convergence.*

Dr. Pert is a modern scientist with a sense of humor and an open mind about the ancient science and wisdom of chakras. And she's not the only one! An on-line search of science and chakras brings up a lot of interesting sites and information about many other 21st century scientists who are making the connection between this ancient wisdom and modern science. So when our family and friends try to tell us that we're wasting our time learning about and balancing our chakras, we can smile and quote Dr. Pert.

# SECTION SEVEN

# AWARENESS + INCREASED VIBRATIONS = SPIRITUAL GROWTH

# Chapter Eighteen: Are We Really Evolving?

Are we really evolving? How can we tell? Our lives are not all flowers and candy and cake, yet based on what we've learned from the GG, it's this way so we can learn, grow, and move forward—think *windows of opportunity* and *relationship villains*. We hear the words *vibration, awareness and evolution* a lot, but what do they really mean to us?

Our souls are comprised of life-force that contains the imprint, knowledge, and historical record of all of our experiences in all of our lifetimes. They also contain and carry the imprint and intent for our current incarnation. Olexeoporath dictated the following on this subject:

Ole: ***Your soul is energy, your higher self is energy, and the Source is energy. Raising your vibrations is a matter of altering your energy. Some are of a higher vibration than others, yet all can raise their vibrations through thought and action.***

Raising our vibrations and evolution—these things are really about our soul. Our soul evolves as we raise our vibratory levels, and we raise our vibratory levels through our thoughts and actions.

**Let's Talk About Vibrations**

In his book, *The Life Beyond Death*, medium Arthur Ford, who also channeled information to Ruth Montgomery after he passed over in 1971, had the following to say about vibrations:

*When we consider the vast multitude of significant vibrations [i.e., x-rays, radio waves, electromagnetic waves, etc.] which surround us at all times and of which we are totally unaware, we see how ridiculous it is to imagine that our five senses give us anything like an accurate picture of the universe we live in. Yet our materialistic scientists would have us think that these, and only these, are the sole source of data from which to derive comprehension! This matter of vibrations is important to me. I am convinced that becoming aware of the next stage of existence beyond the earth biosphere is very largely a matter of becoming its vibrations.'*

═✦═

This "raising our vibrations stuff" isn't new; Ford's words were written nearly half a century ago. When it comes to raising our vibrations, we know that it means that the rate or frequency of our vibrations is raised; however, often we feel like since we can't *see* it happening, it's not *really* happening. My sentiment here is that many of us just don't know what to look for, and that while we might not see a change, most of us will *feel something* as our vibrations rise. In his perceptive and insightful blog (*The Inner Voice*), Jeffrey Marks, radio show host and author of the book, *Your Magical Soul: How Science and Psychic Phenomena Paint a New Picture of the Self and Reality*, wrote the following about what it's like to feel our vibrations rise:

*Now, you might think that in raising [your] vibration you should feel something vastly different from your normal vibration—like you're sitting there, and all of a sudden you should feel like you have a rocket pack strapped to your back. Sorry to say this doesn't happen. But when you reach a good meditative state and with enough awareness, you can actually feel a rapid pulsation go up and down the core of your body through your chakras—it is about double the speed of your heart rate—and you will also notice your breathing is smooth and equal in terms of time spent inhaling and time spent exhaling. This pulsation, now that I think about it, does extend to your skin, too, as I have felt a buzzing sensation across my epidermis during these moments of awareness.*

However, if you don't feel this rapid pulsation, that doesn't mean you haven't raised your vibration, it just means that you haven't got an awareness of it just yet. [ www.jeffreymarks.blogspot.com/]

═✦═

Speaking for myself, I tend to feel a kind of vibrational buzzing or hum in my ears that the GG tells me is a type of energy signal that's giving me a little bump up in frequency. I'm sure that it's different for all of us. There is no right or wrong way to perceive an energy boost, but if we pay attention, we'll discover what our individual signal is. Becoming aware of our vibrations being raised is a good thing, and something we want to watch for because it tells us we're making progress and motivates us to continue doing the things we're doing to move forward. For example:

The *higher our vibration*, the easier it is for us to connect with our Higher Self.

The *clearer our connection* to our Higher Self, the better able we are to move past ego.

As we move past ego and enjoy a clearer connection to our Higher Self, the better able we are to receive understandable and *comprehensible guidance* so that we can make better decisions.

*Better decisions* allow us to learn and grow spiritually, and that, in turn, allows us to *develop and evolve*.

Let's talk a little bit about exactly what it means to raise our vibrations. I like the way hypnotherapist, healer, and founder and director of the Center of Hypnotherapy, Marilyn Gordon (www.marilyngordon.com), describes it:

You are made of electromagnetic energy, and like a magnet, you bring to yourself things, people and events that match the rate of your vibration. So to bring in good fortune, love and happiness and to send those out to the world as well, you want to create as powerful a force-field in your being as you can.

The ways that Marilyn suggests we can create this powerful force-field of what is actually positive energy and raise our vibrations are amazingly similar to what the GG talks about in both *Windows* and *Vibrations*. As you'll see below, both the GG's and Marilyn's suggestions revolve around keeping our thoughts, words and actions as positive as we can:

- **See the advantage of everything**. This means that you look for the positive potentials in everything.
- **Stand back and observe** rather than judge people, things and events. This gives you the chance to take the negative spin off things and just to observe them as they are.

- **Cultivate gratitude** and give thanks for all you have and all you are.
- **Watch the ways you speak to yourself** and vow to be more kind.
- **Live with the possibility that a miracle could happen** for you—and re-paint the vision of your possible future.
- If you can **see how your worries are negative thoughts about the future**, then you can promise yourself to transform your thinking.

What Marilyn says makes sense. What the GG say makes sense. After meditating and contemplating about what it means to raise our vibrations, my thought is that through awareness we *can* become better and nicer people; in this way, we will continue to raise our vibrations and evolve. Even if we're already nice people, which I'm sure is the case, we can consciously take ourselves and 3D Earth to the next level, and the next level after that, and so on—and that, my dear friends, is evolution.

Some say evolution isn't happening because our physical bodies haven't changed since what? Prehistoric times? I say, "So what?" Our bodies may stay the same, but we are witnessing the evolution of our souls—and this is where awareness comes into play.

**Awareness**

My observations regarding awareness are simple, and I don't see anything difficult about the task of improving our awareness. It's something we can put our minds to and see immediate results.

Awareness is directly related to being awake, perceptive, and sensitive to what's going on around us and especially, what's going on *inside* us. It's about our feelings when we see or read about things that are happening in our own little world and the world at large. It also has a lot to do with how we accept, absorb and apply new information. Being open to new ideas absolutely facilitates the expansion of our individual awareness. And we all know that because we're intricately connected, when one of us steps up our awareness, the rest of us will follow.

There was a time in all of our lives when we were not aware of reincarnation, yet that didn't mean that reincarnation wasn't taking place. We might not be aware of the electricity entering our appliances, but it most assuredly does. As we learn and grow and become more awake and sensitive to what's happening around us, we'll react to our new awareness and take the action that will raise our vibrations.

It's my feeling that awareness builds on itself and once we start on the path of awareness, it increases exponentially. This is why so many of us suffer so much when we read the newspaper or watch the news. Our vibrations are at a level that we are much more attuned to the suffering that's going on in the world, and as our awareness levels increase, so does our sensitivity to our perceived injustices in the world. The good news is that this awareness, this wakefulness, this sensitivity is what is going to take us to the next level, and we have the tools to help us get there.

It also seems to me that with awareness comes greater responsibility. We've talked throughout this book about putting on our **BIG** Lightworker pants and taking responsibility for our own spiritual growth and communication with Spirit. With increased awareness also comes increased responsibility to reach out and help each other and our planet. We're evolving. Don't doubt it for a minute. The fact that it seems slow to us, and we don't see any physical evidence of it means nothing. Our souls are evolving, and our job as Lightworkers on 3D Earth is not over.

# Chapter Nineteen: Congratulations!

Yea! You made it all the way through this book, and if you did the exercises and meditations, you've got a great foundation to forge ahead and discover the patterns, scripts, villains and windows that are part of your personal spiritual evolution. You know exactly what to do to raise your vibrations and grow spiritually, and you know you are not alone. Spirit is always with you and waiting to converse with you, and you know how to initiate and continue contact.

This being awake and being aware may be challenging, I think, but isn't this why we began our spiritual journeys? We wanted the truth of our existence. We wanted to know why things are the way they are. That famous Jack Nicholson line, "You can't handle the truth" echoed in my mind as the early chapters of this book were dictated by the GG. I don't think it was so much that I *couldn't* handle the truth; I think it was more that I just plain didn't like a lot of what the GG dictated. It shook me to my core to learn that I would not transition to 5D Earth as Sherri Cortland, and I wasn't *in love* with the idea of being a *nerve ending* for the Source. Eventually, it sank in that I am and we all are part of the Source. Even if I'm not particularly in love with this idea, I still want to know the *truth* of our existence, and I'm told that there's much more new information to come.

We've worked so hard, and we've raised our energies, our frequencies, and our vibrations to the point where information that's more *difficult to digest* is coming through to us. We're *way beyond* learning about reincarnation, karma, and life after death. Through many wonderful channels, Spirit is building on what we've already been given and providing us with more and clearer information about who we *really* are. Congratulations! We've earned the right to our truth. Now that we've got our **BIG** Lightworker pants on, we can expect more awakenings as we continue to evolve. Can we handle the new information we're currently receiving and what's still to come? Yes—because we're Lightworkers, and our Spiritual Toolbox is full! Now let's celebrate all the great and wonderful things we've done to get to where we are today, and here are three powerful words from Jeremy to send us on our way:

***"Go in Peace."***

# Addendum I: Authors, Mediums, & Teachers

Shirley Battie
Author, Spiritual Healer, Clairvoyant, Teacher
www.little-owl.org

Dolores Cannon
Author, Hypnotherapist
www.ozarkmt.com

Theresa Caputo
Psychic Medium
www.theresacaputo.com

Marilyn Gordon
Hypnotherapist, Healer, Found of the Center of Hypnotherapy
www.marilyngordon.com

Linda Howe
Center for Akashic Records

Lori Carter
Akashic Record Practitioner; Karuna & Reiki Master
www.blissfulawakenings.com

Edgar Cayce
Medium & Healer
Association for Research & Enlightenment (ARE)
www.edgarcayce.org

Chip Giller
Author
www.grist.org

Dr. Bruce Goldberg
Hypnotherapist & Akashic Records Expert
www.drbrucegoldberg.com

Judy Hall
Author, Astrologer, Psychic, Healer
www.judyhall.co.uk

Paige Hall-Ferraro
Psychic, Medium, Reiki Master, Crystal Healer, Teacher
www.paigehallferraro.com

Thích Nhất Hạnh
Author, Buddhist Monk, Poet, Scholar, Teacher, Peace Activist
www.plumvillage.org

Linda Howe
Teacher of the Pathway Prayer Process
Center for Akashic Studies
www.lindahowe.com

Craig Howell
Author, Artist, Channeler, Composer
www.cdbaby.com

Irene Lucas
Author, Editor, Producer, Teacher, Metaphysician
http://www.theuniverseislistening.com/

Jeffrey Marks
Author, Radio Show Host
www.jeffreymarks.com

Kim Masoner
Blogger
www.secondact.com

Ruth Montgomery
Author, Channeler
www.ruthmontgomerywritesagain.com

Dr. Pamela Nine
Intuitive Counselor, Spiritual Medium
www.pamelanine.com

Mitchell Osborn
Psychic Medium
www.intuitivemessenger.com

Dr. Candace Pert
Author, Pharmacologist
www.candacepert.com

Katrina Raphael
Author, Crystal Healer
www.webcrystalacademy.com

Sara
Walk-in, Medium, Channeler, Reiki Master, Life Coach
Sara.universal.light@gmail.com

Mary Soleil
Author, Channeler
www.marysoleil.com

Doreen Virtue
Author, Spiritual Doctor of Psychology, Metaphysician, Angel Therapy Practitioner, Teacher
www.angeltherapy.com

Lisa Williams
Psychic Medium
www.lisawilliams.com

Shelly Wilson
Intuitive Medium & Reiki Master
www.shellyrwilson.com

# Addendum II: Referenced Books and CDs

*Crystal Enlightenment Series* by Katrina Raphael

*Convoluted Universe (1-4)* by Dolores Cannon

*Mayan Days of Sound* CD by Craig Howell

*I Can See Clearly Now: How Synchronicity Illuminates Our Lives* by Mary Soleil

*Raising Our Vibrations for the New A*ge by Sherri Cortland, ND

*Spirit Speaks* by Shirley Humphries Battie

*Strangers Among Us* by Ruth Montgomery

*Student Environmental Guide—25 Simple Things We Can Do* by Student Environmental Action Coalition

*The Crystal Bible, a Definitive Guide to Crystals* by Judy Hall

*The Miracle of Mindfulness* by Thich Nhat Hanh

*30 Miracles in 30 Days* by Irene Lucas

*Threshold to Tomorrow* by Ruth Montgomery

*Windows of Opportunity* by Sherri Cortland, ND

*Your Magical Soul: How Science and Psychic Phenomena Paint a New Picture of the Self and Reality* by Jeffrey Marks

# Addendum III: Websites Mentioned

http://today.msnbc.msn.com/id/21601409/ns/today-green/t/its-easy-being-green-ways-help-planet/

http://www.facebook.com/#!/SherriCortlandAuthor.

www.creativespirit.com/aurabook.htm

www.50waystohelp.com

www.Grist.org

www.jeffrymarks.blogspot.com

www.Oprah.com

www.planetgreen.discover.com

www.reiki-for-holistic-health.com/auracolormeanings

www.realsimple.com

www.realmagick/nerve-ganglia.com

www.SherriCortland.com

www.secondact.com/2011/living-green-12-things-you-can-do-to-help-the-planet.com

www.treehugger.com

# About the Author

Originally from New York State, Sherri Cortland lives in Orlando, Florida with her husband, Ted Dylewski and their many cats. In addition to writing books for Ozark Mountain Publishing, Sherri is also the Orlando Metaphysical Columnist for Examiner.com, where publishes new columns twice weekly, and she also shares messages from her Guides on her Facebook Author Page. You can reach Sherri through her website: www.SherriCortland.com.

**www.examiner.com/metaphysical-in-orlando/sherri-cortland**

**www.facebook.com/?ref=tn_tnmn #!/SherriCortlandAuthor**

**Photo by: Heidi Winkler www.HeidiWinkler.com**

"With the release of my first book, Windows of Opportunity, in 2009, I officially came out of the Spiritual Closet and announced to the world that not only do I believe in such things as reincarnation, Karma, and life after death, but that (gasp!) I channel information about these subjects and more from my guides on the other side of the veil. It was scary, very scary, because I have a day job in the business world, and I was worried about what people would say about me, and if I would lose my job. What actually happened is that many people contacted me to say that they have the same beliefs, but didn't know who they could discuss them with, without sounding crazy: The people I thought would have a negative reaction, were stuck in their own closet and started coming out.

Coming out of the closet was the best thing I've ever done, because it allows me to truly be me (at least the *me* I am for this incarnation!), and metaphysics is becoming more and more mainstream as we work together to raise our vibrations and the vibrations of our planet. Together, we are making great progress and I'm so honored to be on this journey with you. It is bright lights of energy connecting and working together that have brought us this far, and recognizing our connection to each other will take us to the next level of our evolution. "

**Special Note:** You can download chapter one of Sherri's three books, *Windows of Opportunity*, *Raising Our Vibrations for the New Age*, and

*Spiritual Toolbox* **free** at www.sherricortland.com; and listen to Sherri's interview on Soul Adventure TV at http://www.youtube.com/watch?v=N2TJniVNq6w.

**Books by Sherri Cortland** (cover photos below):

# Other Books By Ozark Mountain Publishing, Inc.

**Dolores Cannon**
Conversations with Nostradamus, Volume I, II, III
Jesus and the Essenes
They Walked with Jesus
Between Death and Life
A Soul Remembers Hiroshima
Keepers of the Garden.
The Legend of Starcrash
The Custodians
The Convoluted Universe - Book One, Two, Three, Four
Five Lives Remembered
The Three Waves of Volunteers and the New Earth
**Stuart Wilson & Joanna Prentis**
The Essenes - Children of the Light
Power of the Magdalene
Beyond Limitations
Atlantis and the New Consciousness
The Magdalene Version
**O.T. Bonnett, M.D./Greg Satre**
Reincarnation: The View from Eternity
What I Learned After Medical School
Why Healing Happens
**M. Don Schorn**
Elder Gods of Antiquity
Legacy of the Elder Gods
Gardens of the Elder Gods
Reincarnation...Stepping Stones of Life
**Aron Abrahamsen**
Holiday in Heaven
Out of the Archives – Earth Changes
**Sherri Cortland**
Windows of Opportunity
Raising Our Vibrations for the New Age
**Michael Dennis**
Morning Coffee with God
God's Many Mansions
**Nikki Pattillo**
Children of the Stars
A Spiritual Evolution
**Rev. Grant H. Pealer**
Worlds Beyond Death
A Funny Thing Happened on the Way to Heaven
**Maiya & Geoff Gray-Cobb**
Angels - The Guardians of Your Destiny
Seeds of the Soul
**Sture Lönnerstrand**
I Have Lived Before
**Arun & Sunanda Gandhi**
The Forgotten Woman
**Claire Doyle Beland**
Luck Doesn't Happen by Chance
**James H. Kent**
Past Life Memories As A Confederate Soldier
**Dorothy Leon**
Is Jehovah An E.T
**Justine Alessi & M. E. McMillan**
Rebirth of the Oracle
**Donald L. Hicks**
The Divinity Factor
**Christine Ramos, RN**
A Journey Into Being
**Mary Letorney**
Discover The Universe Within You
**Debra Rayburn**
Let's Get Natural With Herbs
**Jodi Felice**
The Enchanted Garden
**Susan Mack & Natalia Krawetz**
My Teachers Wear Fur Coats
**Ronald Chapman**
Seeing True
**Rev. Keith Bender**
The Despiritualized Church
**Vara Humphreys**
The Science of Knowledge
**Karen Peebles**
The Other Side of Suicide
**Antoinette Lee Howard**
Journey Through Fear
**Julia Hanson**
Awakening To Your Creation
**Irene Lucas**
Thirty Miracles in Thirty Days
**Mandeep Khera**
Why?
**Robert Winterhalter**
The Healing Christ
**James Wawro**
Ask Your Inner Voice
**Tom Arbino**
You Were Destined to be Together
**Maureen McGill & Nola Davis**
Live From the Other Side
**Anita Holmes**
TWIDDERS
**Walter Pullen**
Evolution of the Spirit
**Cinnamon Crow**
Teen Oracle
Chakra Zodiac Healing Oracle
**Jack Churchward**
Lifting the Veil on the Lost Continent of Mu
**Guy Needler**
The History of God
Beyond the Source – Book 1

For more information about any of the above titles, soon to be released titles, or other items in our catalog, write or visit our website:
PO Box 754, Huntsville, AR 72740
www.ozarkmt.com

Other Books By Ozark Mountain Publishing, Inc.

**Dee Wallace/Jarrad Hewett**
The Big E
**Dee Wallace**
Conscious Creation
**Natalie Sudman**
Application of Impossible Things
**Henry Michaelson**
And Jesus Said – A Conversation
**Victoria Pendragon**
SleepMagic
**Riet Okken**
The Liberating Power of Emotions
**Janie Wells**
Payment for Passage
**Dennis Wheatley/ Maria Wheatley**
The Essential Dowsing Guide
**Dennis Milner**
Kosmos
**Garnet Schulhouser**
Dancing on a Stamp
**Julia Cannon**
Soul Speak – The Language of Your Body

For more information about any of the above titles, soon to be released titles, or other items in our catalog, write or visit our website:
PO Box 754, Huntsville, AR 72740
www.ozarkmt.com